**Prentice Hall**

# LITERATURE
## Timeless Voices, Timeless

# Teaching Guidebook for Universal Access
## The Literacy Challenge of Diverse Learners

Kate Kinsella, Ed. D

Colleen Shea Stump, Ph.D.

Kevin Feldman, Ed. D.

Prentice
Hall

Upper Saddle River, New Jersey
Glenview, Illinois
Needham, Massachusetts

ISBN 0-13-062857-3

5 6 7 8 9 10    05 04 03 02

# Contents

# Overview
## Universal Access With *Prentice Hall Literature: Timeless Voices, Timeless Themes*

Prentice Hall recognizes that today's classrooms include students with diverse backgrounds and ability levels. Accordingly, the *Prentice Hall Literature* program is structured to provide access to the literature for all students while it develops skills in reading and language arts. The features and components of the program provide both the instructional materials to meet the learning needs of all students and the guidance you need to accommodate those needs. In particular, this *Teaching Guidebook for Universal Access* provides you with the best practices for accommodating those students who may need additional help in reading literature.

The following chart gives an overview of the features and components of *Prentice Hall Literature* that help to address the needs of the diverse population of learners.

| | Features and Components That Support Universal Access |
|---|---|
| **On-level Students** | • In the Teacher's Edition, **Assess Prerequisite Knowledge and Skills** and **Monitor Progress** notes provide support for diagnosing student deficiencies and monitoring progress.<br>• **Background** is provided for every selection in the PRETEACH section of the Teacher's Edition.<br>• The **Time and Resource Manager** before each selection in the Teacher's Edition enables you to see a number of ways that the program uses scaffolding, from the Introduce, Develop, and Conclude spiral of the teaching of the Standards to the customization of instruction levels.<br>• **Reader's Companion** is a consumable supplement that takes an interactive approach to much of the literature in the student book through directed reading questions. |
| **Special Learners** | • **Teaching Guidebook for Universal Access** offers proven strategies for adapting instruction to special learners.<br>• In the Teacher's Edition, **Customized Instruction for Universal Access: Special Needs** provides specific strategies for adapting instructions to the needs of special learners.<br>• **PRETEACH** sections for every selection provide explicit help in guiding understanding.<br>• **Monitor Progress** and **Reteach** notes in the Teacher's Edition provide frequent checks of understanding.<br>• **Adapted Reader's Companion** provides abridged versions of a large number of the selections in the student book with directed, interactive instruction. |

| | |
|---|---|
| | • The following components provide additional practice for special learners:<br>**Selection Support: Skills Development Practice**<br>**Basic Language Skills Reteaching Masters**<br>**Vocabulary and Spelling Practice Workbook** |
| **Advanced Learners** | • Throughout the Teacher's Edition, **For Advanced Readers** and **For Gifted/Talented Students** notes at the bottom of the pages provide opportunities for extending learning.<br>• **Enrichment** notes in the Teacher's Edition provide additional opportunities for extending learning.<br>• **Extension Activities** provide more-challenging writing, speaking, and listening activities for every selection.<br>• **Literary Analysis for Enrichment** provides opportunities for more in-depth literary analysis for every selection.<br>• **Authors in Depth** anthologies provide opportunities for extended exploration of authors featured in the student book. |
| **English Learners** | • **Teaching Guidebook for Universal Access** offers proven strategies for adapting instruction to English.<br>• Throughout the Teacher's Edition, **Customized Instruction for Universal Access: English Learners** notes provide specific strategies for adapting instruction for English learners.<br>• The Teacher's Edition includes **PRETEACH** sections for every selection with notes for explicit teaching.<br>• The student book provides **Vocabulary Development** lessons with integrated spelling instruction in every selection.<br>• **English Learner's Companion** provides abridged versions of a large number of the selections in the student book, with directed, interactive reading notes.<br>• The following components provide additional practice for English learners:<br>**Selection Support: Skills Development Practice**<br>**Basic Language Skills Reteaching Masters**<br>**Vocabulary and Spelling Practice Workbook**<br>• **Listening to Literature** provides professional audio recordings of every selection. English learners can listen as they read along.<br>• **Spanish/English Summaries Audio CD** provides audio summaries for every selection in both Spanish and English. |

## How to Use the Prentice Hall Literature Program

### Achieving Reading Proficiency

The key to students' success in a literature program is their reading proficiency. Students who have reading difficulties can be at risk of falling further behind. Many learning difficulties can be corrected in the regular classroom through special activities and pacing, combined with grouping. Other difficulties, however, may need more focused attention.

For students who are not reading on grade level, you will want to use the **Prentice Hall Reading Achievement System,** which consists of the following components:

- **Reading Diagnostic Test and Improvement Plan**
- **Basic Reading Skills: Comprehensive Lessons for Improvement**
- **Reader's Companion**
- **Adapted Reader's Companion**
- **English Learner's Companion**

Used collectively, the items in this system can make the literature accessible to all students.

**Diagnosing Student Reading Levels** You can use the following components to identify individual students' reading levels and skill deficiencies, as well as to provide necessary reteaching that will move students to grade-level achievement in reading.

1. The *Reading Diagnostic Test and Improvement Plan* provides comprehensive diagnostic tests that assess students' mastery of reading skills. The book also includes charts that will help you map out an improvement plan based on students' performance on the diagnostics.

2. You can use the *Basic Reading Skills: Comprehensive Lessons for Improvement* to give instruction and practice that will enable students to master the skills in which they are deficient. For each skill covered, the following is provided:

    - a lesson plan with direct instruction

    - a teaching transparency

    - a blackline master for student application and practice.

**Reading the Selections With Special Populations of Students** The *Companion* books provide the scaffolding that students of various levels and backgrounds need to read selections in *Prentice Hall Literature.*

1. *Reader's Companion* This consumable book (included in both student and teacher editions in the *Reading Achievement Kit*) contains approximately half of the selections from the student book. Questions followed by write-on lines appear in the margin next to each selection. You can use this book in place of the student book for certain selections to help students read interactively and to assess students' understanding easily. This book is targeted for struggling readers.

2. *Adapted Reader's Companion* This consumable book (included in both student and teacher editions in the *Reading Achievement Kit*) uses the same format and includes the same selections as the *Reader's Companion.* However, the selections are abridged and appear in a larger font size, and the questions are targeted toward special education students. You can use this book as a supplement to or in place of the student book for certain selections

to enable special education students to experience the same literature and master the same skills as on-level students.

3. ***English Learner's Companion***   This consumable book (included in both student and teacher editions in the *Reading Achievement Kit*) also uses the same format and includes the same selections as the *Reader's Companion.* Again, the selections are abridged and appear in a larger font size. The questions and support features are targeted toward English learners. You can use this book as a supplement to or in place of the student book for certain selections to enable English learners to experience the same literature and master the same skills as on-level students.

## Teaching the Selections in the Textbook

**Planning to Teach Each Selection**  Prentice Hall provides the following planning tools to help you prepare to teach each selection:

- **Teacher's Edition**  The *Teacher's Edition* provides a lesson plan for every selection or selection grouping.

- **Resource Pro CD-ROM**  The lesson plans from the *Teacher's Edition* are available in electronic format on the *Resource Pro.* The plans can be modified as necessary.

**Preparing Students to Read the Selections**  The "Preparing to Read" pages that precede each selection in the student edition

- provide necessary **background** for reading the selection;
- teach **literary elements** appropriate to that piece of literature;
- provide a **reading strategy** that students apply to the selection;
- introduce **vocabulary** words from the selection.

You can use the following support materials to teach the "Preparing to Read" pages:

1. *Teacher's Edition*  The *Teacher's Edition* provides a direct-instruction script for preparing students to read the selection and indicates how and when to utilize other ancillaries at this stage.
2. *Interest Grabber Videos*  The *Interest Grabber Videos* are an optional enrichment resource that are used to motivate students to read the selection and/or to provide background information. There is a video segment for every selection or selection grouping in the student book.
3. *Literary Analysis and Reading Transparencies*  These transparencies are teaching aids that you can use to introduce the literary elements and reading strategies that are taught with each selection.

*Directing Students Through the Selection*  Within the student book, the following features appear in the margin beside each individual selection to help direct student reading:

- **Reading Strategy questions** help students apply the strategy.

- **Literary Analysis questions** help students see how the featured literary elements are used in the selection.

- **Reading Check questions** check students' basic comprehension.

- Definitions and pronunciations of **vocabulary words** are provided.

- **Literature in Context** features provide important background information for students at point of use.

In addition, you may draw from the following components to help direct students through each selection:

1. **Teacher's Edition** The *Teacher's Edition* provides direct-instruction scripts for guiding students through the selection and applying the standards being taught.

2. *Listening to Literature Audiotapes* and *CDs* These components feature professional recordings of every selection in the student book. To support student reading, you can play the selections, in full or in part, before students read them.

3. *Spanish/English Summaries Audio CD* Audio summaries are provided for every selection in both Spanish and English. You can play these selections for struggling readers, special education students, and English learners prior to having them read.

4. *Reader's Companion* The directed reading notes with the selections in this consumable book provide additional scaffolding for struggling readers. You can use this book as a supplement to or in place of the student book for certain selections to help students read interactively and to assess students' understanding easily.

5. *Adapted Reader's Companion* The directed reading notes with the selections in this consumable book provide additional scaffolding for readers who are significantly below grade level. The selections are abridged and appear in a larger font size, and the questions are targeted toward special education students. You can use this book as a supplement to or in place of the student book for certain selections to enable special education students to experience the same literature and master the same skills as on-level students.

6. *English Learner's Companion* The directed reading notes with the selections in this consumable book provide additional scaffolding for English learners. This book uses the same format and features as the *Reader's Companion*. Again, the selections are abridged and appear in a larger font size. You can use this book as a supplement to or in place of the student book for certain selections to enable English learners to experience the same literature and master the same skills as on-level students.

**Reviewing and Assessing** After each selection, the student book offers the following features to review the selection and assess student understanding:

- **Critical Thinking questions** cover the full range of critical thinking skills from recall to synthesis. Scaffolded to move students from one skill to the next, these questions help students to apply the skills in analyzing what they have just read.

- **Literary Analysis questions** enable students to apply what they have learned about literary elements.

- **Reading Strategy questions** assess students' mastery of the reading strategy.

These features are supported by the following components:

1. *Formal Assessment*  This booklet provides you with a test for every selection or selection grouping. The tests assess all skills taught with the selection and consist of multiple-choice and essay questions.
2. *Open-Book Tests*  This component provides you with an alternative test for every selection. The tests consist of multiple-choice and short answer questions, questions for extended response, questions based on graphic organizers, and opportunities for oral response.
3. *Test Bank Software*  The Test Bank Software contains all of the tests in the preceding two components. Tests can be customized to specific objectives, difficulty levels, and question types.
4. *Got It! Assessment Videos*  You can use these videos as part of a whole-class activity to check students' comprehension of a selection.

## Integrating Language Arts Skills

Once the class has finished analyzing a selection, you can integrate the following instruction and practice, which appears in the student book:

- **Vocabulary Development lesson,** including instruction and practice in spelling, word parts, and new vocabulary acquisition
- **Grammar skills lesson** with practice
- **Writing lesson** with complete process instruction
- **Listening and Speaking activity**
- **Research and Technology activity**

The following components provide additional instruction and practice:

## Teaching and Assessing the Writing Lesson

1. **Writing Models and Graphic Organizers on Transparencies** You can use these transparencies to instruct students on how to complete the writing lesson. Point-of-use direct-instruction notes in the Teacher's Edition explain when and how to use them.
2. *Writing and Grammar I-Text CD-ROM* This interactive program—referenced in the Teacher's Edition—enables students to complete the writing lesson online and take advantage of interactive graphic organizers, revision checkers, models, and more. E-rater technology provides automatic scoring of student writing.
3. *Performance Assessment and Portfolio Management* This component provides rubrics and models for assessing the writing and listening and speaking activities in the student book.
4. *Extension Activities* Alternative writing, listening and speaking, and other creative activities are provided for each selection. The activities are targeted to varying student ability levels.

## Grammar, Vocabulary, and Spelling Support

1. *Selection Support: Skills Development Workbook* (Teacher's Edition in Teaching Resources box can also be used as blacklines) Reading, Literary Analysis, Grammar, Vocabulary, and Spelling practice worksheets are provided for every selection or grouping. This workbook provides ample practice and reinforcement opportunities for language arts skills development.
2. *Vocabulary and Spelling Practice Book* Students who need even more reinforcement can use this book for extra practice.
3. *Writing and Grammar I-Text CD-ROM* The CD-ROM gives students access to interactive grammar instruction and thousands of practice exercises that are automatically graded for teachers.

## Providing Enrichment

The following components provide opportunities for enrichment:

### Extended or Independent Reading

1. *Prentice Hall Literature Library of Novels, Plays, and Nonfiction* This collection of novels, plays, longer nonfiction works, and anthologies offers ample opportunities for extended or independent reading. The books are accompanied by study guides.
2. *Prentice Hall Literature Library of Anthology Collections* This collection of anthologies—each having a specific focus, such as African American Literature, Nonfiction, or Workplace Writing—provides additional opportunities for extended or independent reading. The books are accompanied by study guides.
3. *Resources for Teaching Novels, Plays, and Literature Collections* This is a collection of transparencies, tests, graphic organizers, and other resources you can use in teaching longer works.
4. *Videotape Library* These full-length feature dramatizations of major literary works can be used to supplement and extend the coverage of novels and plays.
5. *Authors In Depth* For each grade level, an *Authors In Depth* anthology provides the opportunity for extended study of any of ten authors. For each author, additional background, literary selections, discussion questions and activities, and comparative literary analysis are provided. This component is ideally suited for honors-level students.
6. *Literary Analysis for Enrichment* A worksheet for every selection or selection grouping provides the opportunity for extended literary analysis for above-level students.

### Providing Support for Spanish Speakers

The following components provide additional support for Spanish speakers:

1. *Literatura en español* The middle grades editions of this component provide a blend of authentic Spanish-language literature and Spanish translations of selections from the text. Each grade-level book includes thirty pieces of literature, accompanied by questions and activities. The high-school editions provide translations of one selection from each unit of the student textbook, along with summaries in English and Spanish of all the textbook selections or groupings.
2. *Spanish Readings on Audio CD* These CDs contain recordings of all of the selections in *Literatura en español.*
3. *Spanish/English Summaries on Audio CD* These CDs contain summaries in both Spanish and English of all the selections in the English-language student book.

## Teaching Guidebook for Universal Access

Acknowledging the literacy challenge for diverse learners, this *Teaching Guidebook for Universal Access* gives specific techniques, activities, and classroom practices to make each stage of your lesson productive for all students. While it focuses on the needs of three populations—less-prepared students, English learners, and special education students—it promotes success for all students. Using these strategies with your *Prentice Hall Literature* lessons will ensure universal access for all student populations.

# Chapter 1
# Universal Access and the Literacy Challenge of Diverse Learners

## Introduction

> *The number of children in the country who can be classified as diverse learners because of the special circumstances they bring to public education is growing at a pace that currently outstrips educators' abilities to keep up. Unless significant educational changes are made in response to the dramatic changes occurring in classrooms throughout the country, including the development and utilization of instructional strategies that address the needs of diverse learners, the number of children who "fall through the cracks" in public education will continue to rise.[1]*

The 2000 census has confirmed what demographers have been documenting for the past decade: America is more diverse than ever. The diversity of our population is a significant asset to our nation in many ways, but it also places considerable stress on our educational system to effectively accommodate the range of learning needs found in students today. A typical middle-grade classroom includes students who are diverse in terms of their experiential, linguistic, cultural, socioeconomic, and psychological backgrounds. The range of student needs, interests, motivation, and skill levels often presents heightened challenges to both curriculum and instruction. It should be clearly acknowledged that the individual needs of some students require additional specialized support in basic reading skills, English language development, study skills, and behavioral/emotional/social domains. However, the goal of a comprehensive Language Arts program remains the provision of "universal access" for all students to an intellectually rich and challenging language arts curriculum and instruction in addition to whatever specialized intervention may be required.

Universal access occurs when teachers provide curriculum and instruction in ways that allow all learners in the classroom to participate and to achieve the instructional and behavioral goals of general education, as well as of the core curriculum. Teachers will succeed in providing universal access if they teach in heterogeneous, inclusive classrooms and consistently

---

1. Kame'enui, Edward and Douglas Carnine. *Effective Teaching Strategies That Accommodate Diverse Learners.* Upper Saddle River, NJ: Prentice Hall, 1998.

and systematically integrate instructional strategies that are responsive to the needs of typical learners, gifted learners, less proficient readers, English language learners, and students who are eligible for and receiving special education services.

Although each student population represented in the classroom may require specific interventions and supports, these learner populations also share many common characteristics, such as the need to build prior knowledge, the need for systematic vocabulary development, and the need for systematic instruction in strategic reading approaches, to name a few key curricular and instructional areas. Through identification of these shared needs and the implementation of teaching and learning strategies responsive to these needs, the general education teacher, with the support of specialist and other staff, can make significant inroads in designing inclusive lessons that are responsive to the learning and behavioral needs of all learners.

This book provides numerous suggestions to assist teachers in designing English Language Arts lessons that strive for universal access. The suggestions focus specifically on the instructional needs of students who are less proficient readers, students who are English language learners, and students with identified special education needs. Chapter 1 describes the reading process and what it takes to be a proficient reader. Chapter 2 discusses means for designing lessons for the inclusive classroom. Chapters 3 and 4 provide specific recommendations for addressing active participation structures and strategies for passage reading for diverse student groups. Chapters 5, 6 and 7 explore the specific needs of the three focus student populations: less proficient readers, English language learners, and students with special education needs. A summary and appendix of resources are provided to pull all of the ideas together.

It may be helpful to read the chapters in the order they are presented, moving from general considerations to suggestions that address the specific needs of these three student groups. You may also find it helpful to begin with those chapters that address your greatest area of need or interest.

The information in these chapters is designed to provide concrete and easily implemented instructional suggestions for responding meaningfully to the diverse learning needs of students.

# Chapter 2
# The Reading Process:
# What Is a Successful Reader?

A clear consensus has emerged in the field of reading education supporting the notion that reading is a complex process of constructing meaning from text. Successful readers must bring an array of interrelated skills, knowledge, and strategies together in order to understand written English. Skillful intermediate-grade readers are able to decode the words accurately and fluently, connect their meanings to prior knowledge, and continually monitor their emerging understanding as they read. In other words, successful readers are active, thoughtful, and strategic learners able to make meaning from what they are reading.

## Factors That Affect Reading Success

Successful reading in the intermediate grades is largely determined by the elaborate interaction of four factors: learner characteristics, skill and instructional variables, demands of the text, and nature of the classroom environment (see Figure 1). To better understand these elements, we will examine each in turn, as well as the way they interact to affect successful reading.

## Learner Characteristics

Each learner brings unique characteristics to the learning experience. For example, students who are less proficient readers may experience attention and memory issues that make reading especially challenging. English language learners may be highly capable students who, because of limited vocabulary or experiences in their new country, lack the schema for understanding the ideas encountered in text. Students with disabilities may experience cognitive, behavioral/social, and/or physical challenges that make the development of reading skill more challenging.

## Skill and Instructional Factors

Reading success is largely determined by the particular skills an individual reader brings to the reading act. For example, the ability to fluently and accurately decode the words in a given reading selection is a necessary but not sufficient condition for successful reading. In addition, the ability to activate and build prior knowledge along with the related ability to connect what one is reading to existing knowledge are essential for proficient comprehension. Moreover, comprehension is significantly determined by a student's level of English acquisition, vocabulary, and skillful use of various reading comprehension strategies such as summarization or self-questioning.

An essential personal aspect of successful reading is the extent to which a reader is actively engaged in the reading, has a clear purpose for reading, and is interested in the content being explored. Skillful readers have learned helpful mental habits such as perseverance, managing and directing attention, being aware of and monitoring their thoughts and feelings as they read. Skilled readers are active participants in the reading act—reading is not a spectator sport.

Instructional interventions provided in the classroom play a significant role in students' development of these skills. Explicit, systematic instruction in decoding and fluency, the incorporation of activities that build and enhance prior knowledge, the provision of explicit vocabulary instruction, and the direct teaching, modeling, and practicing of comprehension strategies will lead to students' skill development and their enhanced engagement and interest in the complexities of the reading act.

## Text-Based Factors

It is immediately apparent that the types of texts encountered by middle-grade readers vary widely and create different levels of challenge for different readers. Just as the make and model distinguish one automobile from another, text-based factors differentiate one text from another. While some of these factors may be largely cosmetic in nature, others, such as sentence length, novel vocabulary, density of the concepts, or clarity of the organizational pattern, can have a significant influence on reader comprehension. For example, the presence or absence of well-designed reader aids including pictures, charts, graphs, and focus questions can provide additional support to naive readers.

Perhaps the most fundamental distinction in text-based factors affecting reading success is that of narrative (story) reading vs. expository (informational) reading. Expository texts are generally written to inform or persuade the reader using very different organizational patterns from those typically utilized in narratives. For example, information in content-area reading, such as in science and social studies, is often arranged according to structures such as chronological sequence, comparison and contrast, cause and effect, main idea and supporting details, and so forth. Many intermediate-grade students are quite comfortable reading stories but find themselves ill equipped to deal with the demands of informational content-area texts.

## Classroom Environment

The classroom environment affects everything and everyone within it, including the nature of the reading/literacy program. Specifically, the classroom environment can be viewed as composed of both physical and social-psychological dimensions. Research suggests that students learn best in a friendly, respectful setting where

- they feel a sense of safety/order and are comfortable taking risks.
- they understand the purpose of and value the tasks at hand.
- they have high expectations/goals for learning.
- they feel accepted by their teacher and peers.

These general factors are of particular import when thinking about what accounts for successful reading. Middle-grade students will often have significant gaps in their skill, knowledge, proficiency in English, and be self-conscious concerning their lagging literacy.

It is important to be respectful and truthful with students about what it will take to significantly improve their abilities in the Language Arts: It takes PRACTICE, and lots of it. Literacy cannot be "done to" students—it is a collaborative enterprise that is "done with" students. To be sure, teachers provide excellent direct instruction, guided practice, specific feedback, coaching, and more, yet students must understand their roles as active self-directed learners. The intentional design of a caring yet "on purpose" classroom climate creates the condition within which the hard work of improving literacy can take place.

## Figure 1: Factors That Affect Reading Success

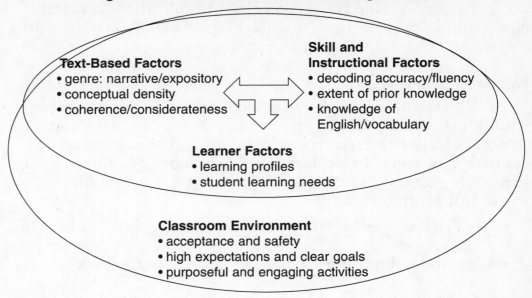

**Text-Based Factors**
• genre: narrative/expository
• conceptual density
• coherence/considerateness

**Skill and Instructional Factors**
• decoding accuracy/fluency
• extent of prior knowledge
• knowledge of English/vocabulary

**Learner Factors**
• learning profiles
• student learning needs

**Classroom Environment**
• acceptance and safety
• high expectations and clear goals
• purposeful and engaging activities

## Summary

Understanding that successful reading comprises a complex interaction of factors—learner, skills and instruction, text, and environment—provides a template for thinking about how classrooms can provide universal access to a rich core curriculum for the diverse range of learners in today's middle-grade classrooms. Middle-grade students need a balanced Language Arts program based on their individual needs, which takes into consideration the factors presented in Figure 1. All students require a firm foundation in fluent/automatic decoding, broad background knowledge of various subjects, ever-expanding vocabularies, coupled with an array of comprehension strategies to fit the purpose for reading as well as the type of text being read.

In the following chapter, we examine strategies for developing lesson plans that support diverse learners in meeting rigorous grade-level standards in the Language Arts. The chapter also presents general considerations for creating inclusive and responsive lessons to meet the needs of less proficient readers, students who are English language learners, and learners with special education needs.

*The truth appears to be quite simply that children* ***need both:*** *a solid skills base that originates indirect instruction with well planned, sequential learning and opportunities to apply learned skills in a wide*

*range of authentic contexts . . . the catch is that application requires competence. Opportunities to apply do not, in themselves, produce the acquisition of new skills. For this, carefully planned instruction and well scaffolded practice is necessary.*
— Andrew Biemiller, University of Toronto

# Chapter 3
# Effective Language Arts Lessons
# for Diverse Student Populations

Teachers craft lessons to include activities and experiences that they consider critical for student participation and learning. At a minimum, lessons generally involve at least these four stages:

Preteach

Teach

Assess

Extend

As teachers craft lessons to reflect these stages, they place emphasis on those stages they consider most critical for their students.

When working with highly diverse groups of students (e.g., students who are English learners, students with special education needs, and students who are less proficient readers), emphasis on the Preteach and Teach stages is critical for a number of reasons:

- Students will most likely need opportunities to build upon and expand their prior knowledge and experiences if they are to understand the concepts presented in the passage.
- Students will most likely require explicit instruction focused on key vocabulary words included in the text.
- Students will most likely need modeling of strategies that will assist them in gaining meaning from the text.
- Students will most likely require additional scaffolding and modeling to be able to access and comprehend the text.

Placing a major emphasis on preteaching and teaching, or "front-loading" your instruction, helps you structure learning for the students to ensure their greater success. In fact, you may want to plan to spend 65% of your instructional time "front-loading" your instruction, spending that time on vocabulary development, building background knowledge, and explicitly teaching students strategies for actively engaging with the text. Consider it an investment in preparing students for encountering and handling the text. By front-loading, you are preparing students for what is to come as well as teaching them generalizable strategies that they can transfer to other academic settings.

Jean Ciborowski, in describing techniques for using textbooks with students who cannot read them, talks about what proficient and less proficient readers do when they approach text:

| Less proficient readers | Strong readers |
|---|---|
| • do not establish a purpose for reading text. | • adopt a strategic stance (e.g., they establish a purpose for reading). |
| • are not active, strategic readers. | • actively monitor their comprehension. |
| • do not apply comprehension breakdown strategies | • read to find out more.[1] |

By attending to the behaviors and strategies of proficient readers and incorporating them into instruction to nurture and teach these approaches to reading, the teacher focuses on the Preteach and Teach phases of instruction and assists students in becoming active, engaged, strategic readers.

The remaining two phases—Assess and Extend—are important for these students as well, but in general preparing students for learning through emphasis on the Preteach and Teach segments of lessons will reap significant gains for these students.

## The Four Phases of Instruction

Each phase of a lesson—Preteach, Teach, Assess, and Extend—is essential to the overall lesson and student engagement and learning. The phases may overlap or occur in a different order, but generally, they are present in all effective lessons. Each of these phases is briefly described in the box in terms of how each is incorporated into a Language Arts lesson. The final column lists suggestions of what to include consistently in each lesson phase.

---

1. Ciborowski, Jean. *Textbooks and the Students Who Can't Read Them: A Guide to Teaching Content.* Cambridge, MA: Brookline Books, 1992.

| Phase | Description | Critical Elements |
|-------|-------------|-------------------|
| **Preteach** | The teacher introduces the topic and prepares students for the text. | • Building on prior knowledge by providing or eliciting background information on the topic.<br>• Preparing the students for the topic by outlining, mapping, and summarizing the "big ideas" of the text.<br>• Providing explicit vocabulary instruction that focuses on critical words for understanding text meaning.<br>• Motivating students to engage with the text.<br>• Setting a purpose for reading the text. |
| **Teach** | The teacher models approaches for actively engaging with text to gain meaning. | • Selecting and modeling of reading strategies that take into consideration student learning needs.<br>• Scaffolding student learning.<br>• Monitoring student understanding and engagement.<br>• Providing multiple opportunities for teacher-student and student-student interactions.<br>• Ensuring student accountability.<br>• Building in and teaching classroom routines to support positive behavior. |
| **Assess** | The teacher formally checks for student understanding. | • Frequently checking-in with students to ensure understanding.<br>• Including systematic means for monitoring student understanding and performance. |
| **Extend** | The teacher provides activities that challenge students to apply passage information in a new way or to a new situation. | • Helping students make links between their prior knowledge and knowledge gained from text.<br>• Having students take information learned and apply it to their lives, or to a new situation. |

## Developing Effective, "Front-Loaded" Lessons to Ensure Universal Access

Below are questions you may want to consider when preparing lessons for the inclusive classroom. These questions will prompt you to consider how you will ensure universal access in the lesson. Again, pay special attention to the questions under the Preteach and Teach segments. These represent critical understandings for students if they are to comprehend the ideas and text they are presented with during the lessons.

| Phase | Critical Elements |
|-------|-------------------|
| **Preteach** | • What topic information do the students already know? What information or experiences do I need to provide for them to be able to understand the "big ideas" of the text they are going to read?<br>• What information do I need to present to students in either graphic or outline form to help them grasp the main ideas of the passage and prepare them for what they will be reading?<br>• What are the most important, high-utility words that all students must know and understand from the passage? How will I teach those words? Also, what will I do during the reading of the passage to link this instruction to the text?<br>• What can I do to get students interested in reading the text?<br>• What will I do to help students establish a purpose for reading the text? |
| **Teach** | • Given the passage, what types of strategies will the students need to support their comprehension (e.g., skimming, identifying main ideas and supporting details, predicting, rereading)?<br>• What kind of scaffolding will students need to understand the text? Do I need to stop and paraphrase at key points in the text? Do I need to call students' attention to key concepts as they are presented?<br>• What type of student-to-student activities have I included in this lesson component (e.g., large group activities, small group and paired learning activities)?<br>• What type of teacher-to-student activities have I included in this lesson component beyond my asking and answering questions (e.g., one-on-one clarification, asking for individual votes or responses to questions)?<br>• What mechanisms have I included to ensure student accountability (e.g., requiring students to take notes, to write and compare predictions with text, to respond to questions asked of the group through voting and response cards)? |
| **Assess** | • Have I prepared questions that will allow me to tap into student understanding?<br>• What types of activities, beyond teacher questions, will I use to check for student understanding (e.g., think-pair-share activities, response cards and voting, writing of summaries or questions about confusion points, numbered-heads together)?<br>• How will I systematically check for student understanding? How will I incorporate these suggestions throughout the lesson?<br>• How will I provide opportunities for students to assess each other's learning?<br>• How can I ensure that students are made accountable for their own learning? What techniques do I need to teach for them to become self-evaluators and self-monitors? |
| **Extend** | • What activity have I included that challenges students to form links between their prior knowledge and knowledge gained from text?<br>• What activity have I planned that requires students to take information learned and apply it to their own lives, or to a new situation? |

## Instructional Considerations for Universal Access

Students who are less proficient readers, English language learners, and students with identified disabilities will most likely require additional adaptations and modifications during instruction if they are to actively participate and achieve in Language Arts lessons presented in the general education classroom.

### General Considerations

The following is a basic list of instructional considerations that can be applied across all four phases of instruction.

- **Clarify behavioral expectations** for the lesson. Students need to understand the parameters within which they are working.

- **Provide time for students to collect their thoughts** before having to speak. You may want to ask a student a question and then pause and count to 10 before you assist the student in responding. You may also want to ask the student a question, state that you want him/her to think about it, and indicate that you will be back for the response in a minute. Go on to another student, and then return to the student for his/her response. Another possibility is to tell students the questions that you will be asking during tomorrow's class in order to give them time, overnight, to prepare their responses. These suggestions can be very helpful for a student experiencing a language disability or for a student who uses an alternative, augmentative communication device.

- **Write all assignments on the board** so that assignments are given both verbally and visually.

- **Use visuals throughout the lesson.** Outlining key ideas, writing key phrases and vocabulary on the overhead projector or board, or putting notes on the overhead projector or board are critical supports for many students. You may want to provide some students, with a copy of your overheads or notes ahead of time so that they can follow along. For other students, make a partial or blank copy of the graphic or outline you will be using and require students to write in key information as it is discussed. It is very helpful if you model this completion/filling-in procedure for students. It also helps them to overcome problems with spelling or capturing complex ideas using a few words.

- **Assist in time management.** When requiring students to complete projects, or long-term assignments, provide a calendar that breaks down requirements by due dates. Go over the checklist with the students and monitor their use of the checklist and task completion as the assignment proceeds. Many students will experience significant difficulties in self-managing the time needed to complete complex and long-term assignments.

- **Schedule opportunities for preteaching and reteaching** key concepts, vocabulary words, and skills. Students will most likely need more than one opportunity to gain understanding and fluency. Preteaching and reteaching could be done in small groups while other students are working on an independent activity; you could also collaborate with a paraprofessional or the special education support staff to provide this support.

- **Consider alternative means for demonstrating understanding.** Think beyond the common modes of reading and writing. Students could present information orally, create a poster or visual representation of work, tape-record their ideas, or act out their understanding. These activities take into consideration "multiple intelligences" and can provide access for all learners in the classroom.

- **Have students begin all work in class.** Prior to class dismissal, check to ensure that each student has a good start and understands what is expected.

- **Consider setting up a homework hotline** using voicemail or e-mail. Homework assignments could be posted and easily accessed by parents and students outside of school hours.

- **Build fluency** by including classroom strategies such as the following:

  1. Paired reading for less than 5 minutes a day

  2. Listening to individual students read, working with 1 or 2 students a day for 2 minutes or so each

  3. Providing books and passages on tape, and having students read along with the tape

  4. Incorporating repeated readings that involve students reading the same passage a number of times

  5. Choral reading

- **Build vocabulary** by teaching the meaning of prefixes and suffixes *(see pages 46-47, 57)*. Also, focus on synonyms and antonyms of words and have students define the words in their own words.

- **Explicitly teach note-taking skills.** Model note-taking as you present information to the classroom. Collect and review the students' notes and provide suggestions for improvement.

- **Use recorded readings.** Some students can benefit from the use of books on tape. One caution: Be sure that students are actively engaged and following along as they listen to the tape. It may be helpful to incorporate a number of the tools previously suggested (e.g., maps, outlines, study guides) for reading activities involving books on tape.

- **Balance student-focused and directed with teacher-focused and directed activities.** Students who are less proficient readers, English language learners, and students with disabilities will often require explicit instruction and modeling. Student-focused activities may assist students in gaining numerous skills, but they need to be balanced with teacher-directed lessons that provide explicit instruction provided by the teacher. Clearly stating expectations, modeling what students are to do, providing examples of finished products, and explicitly teaching vocabulary words, reading comprehension strategies, and strategies for approaching text in a strategic, active way are necessary for these students' success. Other students can benefit from this explicitness of instruction as well. Being explicit does not mean "watering down" or "dumbing down" the curriculum; it means making it explicit so that all students can access it.

### Considerations for Each Lesson Stage

In addition to these general considerations and suggestions, each lesson stage presents unique challenges for teachers. Here are some suggestions for ensuring universal access throughout your lessons.

### Phase 1: Preteach

- In small groups or pairs, have students discuss what they already know about the topic presented in the passage. Circulate among the groups/pairs and record key ideas from each. Present these ideas to the larger group.

- Pose questions that are true or false based on passage content. Have students indicate, either in writing or by voting, their evaluation of the item (e.g., holding their thumb up for true, down for false) to gain a quick sense of understanding.

- Before beginning a new unit, have students write, verbalize, or draw what they know about the topic and present this information to peers.

- Ask students to describe how they felt and what they did when they found themselves in a situation similar to that of the main character of the passage.

- Read selected segments of the passage and ask students what they believe the passage will be about.

- Show a video or present pictures linked with the topic of the passage. Ask students to react and to predict what they think the passage will be about.

- Generate a list of questions that pertain to the content of the passage. Have students predict, based on these questions, what they believe the passage will be about. Encourage them to ask questions about ideas they are unfamiliar with.

- Preview the text. Look at and discuss headings, graphics, illustrations, and other elements of the text that provide clues to the content.

- Review the questions to be answered prior to reading the passage. Have students identify the "big ideas" of the passage and what they should be looking for when reading. Have them translate the questions into purposes for reading the text.

- Develop and present an outline or graphic that highlights the key facts, concepts, and vocabulary students will need to understand the passage. Discuss, in detail, the different elements presented in the outline or graphic. Emphasize the "big ideas" and how they relate to one another. Explicitly ask students to look for their ideas when reading.

- Select essential, high-utility words found in the passage and, following the suggestions provided in the segment on vocabulary (*see pages 46–47*), explicitly teach the meaning of these words.

- State a purpose for reading the passage. Tell students what they will learn or why they will be reading the passage (e.g., "We are going to read to find out . . .").

## Phase 2: Teach

- Provide clear expectations. State what you expect the students to do, and model how they are to do it. Review rules.

- Direct and explicit instruction is at the heart of effective teaching:

  "I do it" (model/clarify)

  "We do it" (structure guided practice/feedback)

  "You do it" (structure independent practice activities)

- Describe, model, and have students practice classroom routines (e.g., distributing and collecting materials; moving into and out of small and paired learning arrangements).

- Break up the period by alternating between teacher-dominated and student-dominated activities.

- Try not to engage in oral, paired, or silent reading for more than ten minutes at a time. Bring the group back together as a whole to discuss what was read, or have students stop to complete an activity related to what has been read (e.g., fill out a graphic organizer, answer questions presented in a study guide) to break up and chunk your instruction.

- Provide students time to dialogue with one another and with the teacher throughout the reading of text (e.g., shared pairs, cooperating groups, large groups question/answer and clarification activities).

- Provide multiple practice opportunities when requiring students to attempt new skills or to work with new concepts and vocabulary. For example, when asking students to identify main ideas and supporting details, provide multiple passages for which students complete this activity. Model the approach, have the students attempt the approach, check in with their performance at a mid-point and when finished, and then have the students attempt it with peers or independently.

- Adapt and modify instruction to meet specific learning needs (see information presented in the section on diverse learner characteristics).

- Make tasks authentic to increase motivation and understanding. Make explicit connections between the content and students' lives.

- Have students predict as they read a passage. Have them compare their predictions to the path the author has chosen.

- Have students summarize and clarify as they read.

- Incorporate think-alouds into your instruction. Think-alouds make explicit and audible the thinking processes involved in completing a task so students can hear and experience them.

- Have the students map or outline the text as it is being read. You can provide complete, partial, or blank maps or outlines, based on students' needs. Students may complete them independently, in small groups, or pairs, or the classes, under the teacher's direction, may complete them as a group, with the teacher modeling the recording of the information using the overhead projector or chalkboard.

- Provide a study guide to go along with the passage being read. The study guide can include guiding questions, vocabulary activities, and mapping/outlining activities to support student understanding. They may be completed in formats similar to those suggested when using maps and outlines.

## Phase 3: Assess

- Make assessment an integral and ongoing part of your teaching.

- Incorporate multiple assessment formats (e.g., multiple-choice and true/false quizzes, essay questions, projects, presentations).

- Have students be responsible for part of the assessment of their learning. Students can reflect on and write about what they have learned; students can compare pre- and post-projects and identify what they have learned and how their work has changed; or students can complete checklists and surveys that ask them to evaluate their work and understanding.

- Incorporate authentic assessment activities as appropriate (e.g., when the goal is for the student to be able to write a letter, have the student write a letter to a real person rather than having them provide correct punctuation for a teacher-developed letter written to someone the student does not know).

## Phase 4: Extend

Students who are less proficient readers, English language learners, and students with disabilities are also highly capable students who can actively engage in extended activities, if these activities are structured by necessary supports.

Many of the suggestions provided under "Teach" apply here as well. With explicit presentation of expectations and instructions, paired with examples of previous student projects, these students can be successful. There are, however, some considerations when planning Extend activities for these student groups:

- Ensure that these activities require students to apply core understandings. The activities should challenge students to take the information learned from the text and use it in new and novel ways, or to apply it to a new situation.

- Ensure that these activities are connected with the students' lives.

- Ensure that these activities are not "busy work" but represent real learning and goal achievement.

### Summary

"Front-loading" instruction by providing extensive instruction during the Preteach and Teach phases of lessons provides a foundation for student participation and achievement. It also provides students with opportunities to practice skills, to build schema before encountering text, and to interact with vocabulary prior to reading. In addition to "front-loading" instruction, identify the unique learning needs of your student group and incorporate instructional techniques that will support their active participation and achievement to ensure universal access for all learners, including those who are less proficient readers, English language learners, or who have special education needs. Also, employ systematic means for monitoring and evaluating student understanding and use this information to guide your instruction and incorporation of adaptations and modifications into future lessons.

# Chapter 4
# Structures for Active Participation and Learning During Language Arts Instruction

## A Rationale for Structured Engagement and Participation

English Language Arts discussions and activities are often less than democratic or engaging in heterogeneous secondary classrooms. More academically prepared and confident learners can tend to dominate both unified-class discussions and small-group activities. Students who are at all insecure about their subject-matter preparation or English language skills may elect to remain passive, waiting for the classmates who are always ready to respond to speak up. Furthermore, English language learners and other students who are not strong auditory processors need considerable wait time to process a question and frame an answer, but this instructional support is rarely factored into traditional class discussions. Similarly, many competent yet highly analytical and reflective learners require additional processing time and tranquility to incubate after being presented with a problem or question. If impetuous or loquacious students are regularly allowed to blurt out answers, other more reflective or reticent participants are left with little time or incentive for critical thinking and engagement. When this instructional dynamic is revisited on a routine basis, less assertive or proficient students are denied the interaction and affirmation that will encourage them to take greater social and academic risks and make vibrant classroom contributions.

## Classroom Participation Structures

There are a number of strategies teachers can manageably integrate into their daily Language Arts lessons to encourage more active and productive learning from all students. These participation structures involve students in dynamic interaction and construction of knowledge by drawing upon a repertoire of oral and written language skills. Each structure, while easy to implement, builds in the conscientious scaffolding necessary for less proficient students to channel their energy and participate more productively in every lesson phase. These structures offer efficient and effective formats for independent seatwork, partner sharing, small group brainstorming and problem solving, and unified class debriefing. Several are adaptations of cooperative structures designed by Spencer Kagan and his colleagues, with a viable research base to support their use in linguistically and culturally diverse classrooms.[1]

Unlike traditional brainstorming and discussion formats, these highly structured activities build in quiet time for independent reflection and recording of thoughts prior to discussion. This "prepared participation" rewards mature reflection rather than spontaneity and builds in a sense of accountability for all students to contribute. Besides creating conditions for more active, responsible learning, the cooperative and task-based nature of these structures helps to promote a safe and supportive context for reticent participants to get their ideas expressed and recognized. The more eclectic range of responses in turn raises the interest level of the class, while preparing students with relevant background knowledge for a subsequent reading or writing task.

Students' confidence and productivity in these interactive structures can be greatly enhanced by instructional "front-loading" in relevant and appropriate language strategies for affirming, seeking clarification, paraphrasing, and so on. Many students, in particular English language learners, will not be familiar with these critical language functions for classroom interaction and learning, as they are used less commonly in casual social interactions on the playground and in the cafeteria. However, the ability to use these communicative strategies is a key to success in the middle-grades Language Arts classroom and other academic and formal social contexts. To support students in comfortably using these strategies, introduce and practice a few new expressions at a time, prior to having students engage in a structure that requires this authentic language. Keep these language strategies posted in the classroom for easy reference during lessons and affirm students' efforts to apply them.

## Language Strategies for Active Classroom Participation

| Expressing an Opinion | Predicting |
| --- | --- |
| I think/believe that . . . | I guess/predict/imagine that . . . |
| It seems to me that . . . | Based on . . . , I infer that . . . |
| In my opinion . . . | I hypothesize that . . . |

---

**1.** Kagan, Spencer. *Cooperative Learning Resources for Teachers.* San Juan Capistrano, CA: Kagan Cooperative Learning, 1992. *See also* Harmin, M. *Strategies to Inspire Active Learning.* Edwardsville, IL: Inspiring Strategy Institute, 1995.

## Asking for Clarification

What do you mean?

Will you explain that again?

I have a question about that.

## Soliciting a Response

What do you think?

We haven't heard from you yet.

Do you agree?

What answer did you get?

## Individual Reporting

I discovered from ____ that . . .

I found out from ____ that . . .

____ pointed out to me that . . .

____ shared with me that . . .

## Disagreeing

I don't agree with you
    because . . .

I got a different answer.

I see it another way.

## Affirming

That's an interesting idea.

I hadn't thought of that.

I see what you mean.

## Paraphrasing

So you are saying that . . .

In other words, you think . . .

What I hear you saying is . . .

## Acknowledging Ideas

My idea is similar to/related
    to ____'s idea.

I agree with ____ that . . .

My idea builds upon ____'s idea.

## Partner and Group Reporting

We decided/agreed that . . .

We concluded that . . .

Our group sees it differently.

We had a different approach.

## Offering a Suggestion

Maybe we could . . .

What if we . . .

Here's something we might try.

## Holding the Floor

As I was saying, . . .

If I could finish my thought . . .

What I was trying to say was . . .

### Whip-around (or Idea Wave)

- Students listen while the teacher poses a question or a task.

- Students are given quiet time to consider what they know about the topic and record a number of possible responses. This may be a simple list of words and phrases or a focused quick-write. It is also helpful to provide students with a series of response prompts to complete prior to being asked to share aloud. In this way, less proficient academic language users will have a linguistic scaffold to bolster their linguistic output along with their confidence in sharing aloud. For example, if students are being asked to make predictions about what will happen in the next chapter of *The Joy Luck Club*, they might be provided with these sentence prompts to complete: I predict that Waverly's mother will be disappointed in/proud of her daughter's behavior because . . .; Based on Waverly's relationship with her mother, I assume that her mother will react very positively/ negatively because . . .

- The teacher whips around the class in a relatively fast-paced and structured manner (e.g., down rows, around tables), allowing as many students as possible to share an idea in 15 seconds or less.

- After several contributions, there tends to be some repetition. Students point out similarities in responses using appropriate language strategies (e.g., My idea is similar to/related to . . .), rather than simply stating that their ideas have already been mentioned. This fosters active listening and validation of ideas.

- The teacher can record these ideas for subsequent review, or have students do a quick-write summarizing some of the more interesting contributions they heard during the discussion.

### Think (write)-Pair-Share (or Private-Partner-Public)

- Students listen while the teacher poses a question or a task.

- Students are given quiet time to first answer the question individually, ideally in writing.

- Students are then cued to pair with a neighbor and discuss their responses, noting similarities and differences.

Students encourage their partners to clarify and justify responses using appropriate language strategies (e.g., How did you decide that?; In other words, you think that . . .).

It is often helpful to structure the roles (first speaker, first listener) and designate the time frames (e.g. "First speakers, you have 90 seconds to share your answers with your partner . . .")

- After rehearsing responses with a partner, students are invited to share with the class.

## Numbered Heads

- Students number off in teams, one through four.

- The teacher asks a series of questions, one at a time.

- Students discuss possible answers to each question for an established amount of time (about 30 seconds to 90 seconds, depending on the complexity of the task).

- The teacher calls a number (1–4), and all students with that number raise their hand, ready to respond.

- The teacher randomly calls on students with the specified number to answer on behalf of their team.

- Students are encouraged to acknowledge similarities and differences between their team's response and that of other teams (e.g., We predicted a very different outcome.; Our reaction was similar to that of Ana's group.).

- The teacher continues posing questions and soliciting responses in this manner until the brainstorming or review session is finished.

## Give One and Get One

- Students listen while the teacher poses a question or a brainstorming task.

- Students are given quiet time to consider what they know about the topic and record a number of possible responses. This may be a simple list of words and phrases or a series of complete sentences.

- Students draw a line after their final idea to clearly delineate their own ideas from those that they are going to gather from classmates.

- Students are given a set amount of time (about 8–10 minutes) to get out of their seats and share ideas with classmates.

After finding a partner, the two students exchange papers and quietly read each other's ideas. They comment upon anything of particular interest on their partner's list or ask for clarification about anything confusing. Students then select one idea from their partner's list and add it to their own, making sure to understand and accurately copy the idea alongside the partner's name, because they may be called upon to share one new idea during the follow-up debriefing session. When one exchange has been completed, students move on to interact with a new partner.

- At the end of the "Give One and Get One" exchange period, the teacher facilitates a unified-class debriefing of ideas. The teacher calls on a volunteer who shares one new idea acquired from a conversation partner, utilizing language for classroom reporting (e.g., "I found out from Alex that . . ."; "Sylvia mentioned that . . ."). The student whose idea has just been reported shares the next idea, gleaned from a different conversation partner. This highly structured debriefing encourages active listening as students are eager to see when their name and idea will be mentioned. Students should strive to share an idea from a classmate who has not yet been acknowledged.

- The teacher records the successive contributions on the board, making sure to write the name of the student next to his/her idea. This relatively random listing can subsequently be restructured in a graphic organizer and used as a springboard to an independent reading or writing task.

### Outcome Statements

- Students in the middle grades often have a difficult time summarizing focal lesson content, monitoring their understanding and use of new strategies, and reflecting critically on their learning. This structure encourages students to review a class session and reflect meaningfully on the day's discussion and activities, while also providing the teacher with productive feedback on instruction.

- The teacher provides students with a series of prompts to complete written "Outcome Statements" about the day's lesson. Possible prompts might include the following:

  I now understand how to . . .

  I was surprised by . . .

  I am beginning to wonder why . . .

  I would like to know more about . . .

  I can see the connections between . . .

  I would like some help with . . .

  I'm becoming more confident about . . .

- Students write two or three detailed Outcome Statements about new insights, observations, or sources of confusion, which could then be shared during a Whip-around or a Think-Pair-Share. Either option could lead into a unified-class summary discussion, with the teacher synthesizing and elaborating where necessary.

- These written reflections can also be turned in to enable the teacher to identify any areas in need of review or clarification. Students who may feel reticent to seek clarification or assistance during a class session are provided with a safe venue for expressing their needs and concerns.

# Chapter 5

## Strategies for Effective Passage Reading During Language Arts Instruction

### But They Can't Read the Text!

A significant challenge to all middle-grade teachers revolves around the problem of what to do about the required core texts that many, sometimes most, of the students cannot independently read—let alone construct sophisticated understanding of the ideas contained within. The following section highlights some practical alternatives that will assist your least prepared readers while productively engaging the most accomplished students in your classroom.

### Common Less Effective Options

**Teacher Reads Aloud:** While reading aloud can be a powerful educational tool for many purposes (e.g. modeling a strategy), it is not recommended as the primary solution to our problem because it renders the students too passive and dependent, with the teacher doing all of the work! When you do choose to use reading aloud as a scaffold for students who can't decode the words, be sure to give them a specific job/role to perform while you are reading, such as listening to answer a question, filling out a graphic organizer of key points, raising a question to pose to the class, and so on.

**Round Robin Reading:** This approach has a litany of shortfalls and is not usually very useful as a whole-class approach to passage reading. For the skillful readers, round robin reading often results in students reading ahead to rehearse their lines, failing to attend to text meanings. In contrast, the below-level readers are dreading their turn, fearing probable public humiliation, likewise not attending to the developing content of the reading.

**Assigning Reading Students Can't Do:** It goes without saying that the practice of assigning the reading of texts students can't read makes little sense and only causes frustration for both teachers and students.

**Limiting Text Reading:** The self-evident result of avoiding necessary practice in reading is, of course, lack of improvement. While demonstrations, simulations, and multimedia-based approaches have their place, students need to engage in large amounts of text reading to become more proficient in this complex ability.

## Productive Alternatives

**Choral Reading:** A common primary grade practice, choral reading can work very well with older readers as well. Choral reading is effective because it requires that each student, regardless of level or proficiency in English, actively engage in attending to the text, while providing a nonthreatening atmosphere in which to practice.

---

**Tips to ensure success with choral reading:**

- Request students to *"Keep your voice with mine,"* to discourage them from racing ahead.

- Pick relatively short passages (e.g., 300 – 500 words).

- Follow with a second silent reading. Now that all students have basic access to the text, a second reading can elicit deeper understanding, supply an opportunity to apply previously taught strategies, answer inductive questions, and so on.

---

**Cloze Reading:** Taken from the cloze assessment process, in which key vocabulary words are left out and readers predict likely sensible words from context, cloze reading involves the teacher's reading aloud and leaving out every 7–10th word, which is then chorally supplied by the student. Cloze reading gives each student a task (follow along carefully and be ready to jump into the breech), allows the teacher to model effective oral reading, and moves a bit more rapidly than choral reading. It is much like a musical duet performed by a masterful teacher simultaneously desiring to model expert performance while providing a chance for the apprentice to practice.

---

**Tips to ensure success with cloze reading:**

- Choose meaningful words to leave out that at least half of the class can read (prepositions and other connecting words do not work well)

- Pick passages of medium length (e.g., 500–1,200 words)

- Expect that students will not pay close attention to the content during their first experience or two with cloze reading (their focus will be on when you are going to stop). Soon, however, they will catch on.

- Occasionally follow cloze reading with a silent reading, as in choral reading (repeated reading is often an excellent first step in "reading to learn").

---

**Silent Reading:** When students are not too far below the level of the text (within 2 grade levels), structured silent reading offers an effective whole-class strategy. The essential element here, as with both choral and cloze reading, is to make sure the students have a job, a task during reading that increases their attentiveness, cognitive focus, and accountability. Reading silently to answer a question previously posed to the class as a whole efficiently meets this goal. Teachers may pose useful questions that the class silently reads to answer. Over time, students are taught to construct a range of questions themselves before such class reading (moving from literal to inferential). After each section is read, engage students in a brief discussion to clarify questions and vocabulary and to ensure common understanding of essential big ideas in the text. (You may choose to guide students in mapping or note taking from the text at this point as well.)

---

**Tips to get the most from structured silent reading:**

- Chunk the text into 1–4 paragraph sections within which students silently read and answer questions.

- Request that anyone who finishes before you convene the discussion go back and reread the section to look for additional details in the text.

- The first few times, model how one thinks while reading to find answers to a question. Think aloud to give students a "window" on this sophisticated cognitive task.

- Invite students to discuss their thinking, as well as their answers, during whole-class discussion. For example, focus on such issues as "How did you know?" or "Why did you think that?"

---

**Structured Partner Reading:** Research has consistently pointed to partner reading as a potent strategy to increase the amount of actual reading students engage in, while providing access for all students to key ideas in the text. Partner reading is an excellent way to ensure that all students are actively engaged in the text and accountable for doing their jobs. It affords the teacher an opportunity for informal assessment via direct observation of how students are dealing with the text (e.g., decoding, fluency, expression, understanding, and so on). Partner reading will work well if most of your students are within 2 grade levels of core texts' level of difficulty. Teachers can also use this same format for increasing strategic reading practice by using different levels of texts based on the reading ability of each pair. For example, student pair numbers 1 and 16 may be reading a novel at eighth grade level, while pair numbers 15 and 30 may be reading a novel at fourth grade level, yet both pairs are practicing the reading strategies (e.g. summarization/paraphrasing) being taught to the whole class.

---

**Tips to get the most from structured partner reading:**
- Rank order students by overall literacy and proficiency in English, placing student #1 with student #16 and so on. Students #1 and #15 are the first readers; #16 and #30 are the first coaches.

### Placing Students for Partner Reading

| Higher Performing Student | Lower Performing Student | Pair |
|---|---|---|
| #1 | #16 | Pair A |
| #2 | #17 | Pair B |
| #15 | #30 | Pair P |

- Ensure that activities are fully reciprocal—students should spend equal time in the roles of reader and coach.
  - Provide specific directions, and demonstrate the roles of reader and coach. (E.g,. "First reader: Whisper-read the first paragraph, coaches follow along, fix mistakes, and ask the comprehension questions.")

**The Reader:**
Reads a paragraph or a page, or reads for a given amount of time. Touching under the words may be helpful if the students have extremely limited literacy.

**The Coach:**
Encourages and supports the reader.
1. If the reader asks for a word, the coach will say the word.
2. If the reader makes a mistake, the coach will correct the error using the following steps:
   a. Point to the word and say, "*Can you figure out this word?*"
   b. If the reader cannot figure out the word in five seconds, say "This word is _____."
   c. Have the reader repeat the word and then reread the sentence.

---

**Why reread the entire sentence?**
- Improve comprehension.

- Practice the word again—read it fluently in context.

- Hold students accountable for reading more carefully.

**Tip for students who simply can't read the text at all**
(too low-level to be partners)
Choral Reading. Place very low readers on a triad. Have one 1 and two 2's. The 2's read chorally, prompting more practice and individual accountability in a safe, nonthreatening atmosphere.

After students have mastered the basic sequence, add various comprehension strategies, such as retelling main ideas after each page or section.
- Summarize/paraphrase. State the main idea in ten words or less. (Using only 10–12 words prompts students to use their own words.)

- Predict and monitor. Reader predicts what will happen next, reads a paragraph/section and then determines if the prediction was accurate, revises as needed, summarizes, and predicts again, continuing for a set amount of time.

## Summary

Passage-reading strategies to accommodate student diversity can be used flexibly in a variety of ways. After spending the necessary time on prereading, vocabulary, and other before-reading or "front-loading" strategies, many teachers find it helpful to begin a challenging passage with more teacher-directed strategies, such as choral and cloze reading. This support provides students a vehicle for getting into the passage, clarifying key big ideas, and in effect, gets them "off on the right foot." At this point, more student-directed strategies might be most appropriate, such as partner reading and/or structured silent reading. In any event, it is the element of careful teacher structuring that provides the key to successful passage reading, using effective teaching practices including choral, cloze, silent, and partner reading in diverse classrooms.

# Chapter 6
# Language Arts Instruction and English Language Learners

The number of immigrant, migrant, and refugee students in the United States who have little knowledge of the English language is growing exponentially. In fact, students who are learning English as an additional language are the fastest-growing segment of the school-age population. While the number of English language learners (ELLs) nationwide has skyrocketed, their academic achievement trails behind that of their native English-speaking peers. National studies of English language learners have shown that they are likely to come from disadvantaged socioeconomic backgrounds, attend low-income schools, and have parents with limited English proficiency. These students are also judged by their teachers to have weaker academic abilities, receive lower grades, and score well below their classmates on standardized tests of mathematics and reading.[1] Moreover, in a large-scale California study, secondary schools reported that even long-term resident ELLs entered high school with only fourth to sixth grade academic competencies.[2]

## Differential Preparation for Second-Language Schooling

Secondary-school curricula are based on assumptions about basic reading and writing skills and elementary subject matter foundations. However, the growing population of secondary English language learners is tremendously diverse, particularly with regard to their educational backgrounds. These students enter U.S. schools with varying degrees of curricular preparation and a vast range of language proficiencies, in English and their native language. At times, it may seem that the one thing these diverse students have in common is the need to accelerate their English language and literacy acquisition in order to participate more fully in their secondary schooling.

Although some have parents with impressive levels of formal education and professional job experiences, many come from less privileged families, challenged by limited functional literacy even in their native language. Newcomers from war-torn regions and rural areas of developing countries are apt to arrive severely under-schooled, with fragmented native language literacy training and weak subject matter foundations.

---

**1.** Moss, M., and M. Puma. *Prospects: The congressionally mandated study of educational growth and opportunity.* Washington, DC: U.S. Department of Education, 1995.

**2.** Minicucci, C., and L. Olsen. "Programs for secondary limited English proficiency Students: A California Study." *Focus,* Vol. 5. Washington, DC: National Clearinghouse for Bilingual Education, 1992.

These youths predictably require compassion, considerable time, and patient modeling simply to adjust to basic school routines and expectations before they can ever begin to concentrate on phonemic awareness lessons, let alone literary analysis.

On the other hand, more fortunate immigrant youths have benefited from rigorous and sustained elementary schooling in their native country and make the transition to American classrooms more effortlessly. Literate in their home language, these second-language learners have already internalized critical scripts for schooling and often function above equivalent grade levels in math or science. However, these traditionally educated newcomers still face a daunting transition to daily instruction in a language they have only begun to study, along with curriculum content, teaching practices, and skills that may not have been emphasized in their native schooling.

Our secondary schools also serve increasing numbers of students who have been raised and educated entirely in the United States but who speak a language other than English at home. These continuing English language learners were either born in the United States or arrived here as very small children. Many of these long-term U.S. residents are not literate in their home language and remain struggling English readers well into the upper grades and beyond. They may demonstrate a comfortable handle on the social domain of both languages, but flounder with grade-level reading and writing tasks.

In summary, with regard to prior schooling, secondary English language learners tend to fall into one of three general and frequently overlapping categories:

(1) Recent adolescent immigrants who have received continuous native language schooling prior to immigration to the U.S. and are prepared with relatively strong academic and study skills to apply to new subject matter

(2) Language minority students continuing into secondary schools from U.S. elementary schools with insufficient English fluency and literacy to compete in challenging academic areas

(3) Immigrant, refugee, and migrant students with sporadic or no prior schooling who consequently enter lacking basic literacy and elementary curricular foundations.

## Second-Language Literacy Development

Statistics on the academic achievement of English language learners demonstrate a dire need for informed attention devoted to literacy, the cornerstone of all academic abilities.

Nonetheless, given the extreme variability in these students' educational histories, they must be offered different pathways to eventual academic success. One approach to literacy instruction will not fit all English language learners. However, the instructional practices outlined in this chapter and throughout this manual should greatly assist them in participating more fully in a heterogeneous secondary Language Arts classroom.

Those with significant gaps in their elementary educational backgrounds will require a thoughtful and sustained literacy intervention program, complemented by a substantive and protracted English language development program. Their acute and compelling academic needs cannot be accommodated solely within the confines of the general education Language Arts classroom, an after-school tutorial, or a reading intervention program.

Similarly, literate and academically prepared newcomers will still need a viable English language development program to enable them to transfer the knowledge and skills they acquired in their native language schooling to the curricula they are studying in the United States. Literate adolescents who are virtual beginners in English will also benefit from a separate reading support class, to help them readily acquire the basic phonology, morphology, and syntax of English, and to more efficiently transfer the reading skills they have already mastered in their native language. Students who can already read relatively fluently in their first language will make an easier transition to English decoding than bilingual classmates who are nonreaders. These literate second-language learners will therefore need to move more rapidly than struggling ELL readers, from initial skill-building lessons that focus on decoding, word recognition, and pronunciation to explicit instruction in comprehension strategies such as prediction, questioning, and summarizing that will help them deal more productively with the reading demands of content-area classrooms.

## Reading in a Second Language

Research findings suggest that reading processes in a second language are not significantly different from those in a first language.[3] For example, both rely on the reader's background knowledge regarding the topic and text structure to construct meaning, and both make use of cueing systems (graphic,

---

[3]. Grabe, W. "Current developments in second language reading." *TESOL Quarterly (1991)*, 25, 375–406.

syntactic, phonological, semantic) to allow the reader to predict and confirm meaning.

While literacy processes in first and second languages may be quite similar, two crucial areas of difference must be addressed. First, initial reading and writing in English will be slower and more painstaking for second-language learners because of their lack of overall fluency. The second-language learner is often in the process of acquiring basic oral language while simultaneously developing literacy skills in English. Limited proficiency in a second language can cause a proficient reader in the native language to revert to poor reading strategies, such as reading word by word. Also, some students may not even have the native language literacy skills to transfer concepts about print and strategies to the second language.

Secondly, ELL students are likely to have less prior knowledge and relevant vocabulary to process new information while reading academic English assignments. Furthermore, readers' background knowledge is often culture-bound and may not match the content needed for a given reading text. ELL students with a limited range of personal and educational experiences on a reading topic will therefore have little to draw upon to construct meaning from a selection even if they are able to accurately decode.

## Academic Language Development

Many adolescent ELL students come to school with sufficient social language for everyday classroom interactions yet are severely lacking in the academic English foundations to tackle a poem or follow the instructions on a standardized test. This is because academic vocabulary is primarily developed through school-based reading and repeated exposure during content-based classroom activities.

The average native English-speaking student enters elementary school with an internalized understanding of the syntax and phonology of English, plus a working vocabulary of several thousand words. This vocabulary base is enhanced each year through new school experiences and reinforced in home and community settings. In striking contrast, the language minority student enters U.S. schooling with a tenuous grasp of the phonology and syntax of the English language, a scant working English vocabulary, and rare opportunities for practice and expansion of this knowledge outside the classroom. As a consequence, they must develop content-specific language and literacy skills along with conceptual foundations, all the while competing with native English-speaking classmates who may also be challenged by grade-level Language Arts curricula, but who at least operate from a relatively firm foundation in basic academic English and years of exposure to high-frequency social English vocabulary.

## Implications for English Language Arts Instruction

A number of implications for instruction can be drawn from these descriptions of the academic language and literacy challenges of ELL students. Novice English readers will require extensive and dynamic instructional "front-loading" in order to effectively grapple with challenging literacy tasks. Teachers all too often concentrate their energies on the damage-control phase, when it becomes clear that students either failed to comprehend or felt too overwhelmed to even try to tackle a reading task. Explaining critical concepts and language after the fact does little to engender reader confidence or competence for the next task. The students may walk away with a better grasp of the plot development in the *The Joy Luck Club* but have no sense of how to proceed with the next chapter. Instead, conscientious literacy mentors essentially "teach the text backwards" by devoting far more instructional time to the preparation and guidance phases of lessons. Since a second-language reader may be approaching an assignment with impoverished background knowledge and weak English vocabulary, it makes sense to concentrate on classroom activities that build strong conceptual and linguistic foundations, guide them into the text organization, model appropriate comprehension strategies, and provide a clear purpose for reading. This responsible preparation will in turn help to create the kind of nurturing affective and cognitive arena that communicates high expectations for their literacy development and encourages them to persist and take risks.

## Instructional Considerations When Preparing Lessons to Support English Language Learners

All of the lesson-planning principles and instructional practices detailed throughout this teacher reference will support ELL students in making strides in their second-language literacy development and in becoming vibrant members of the classroom community of learners. Following are some additional reminders of ways in which you can support ELL students at various stages of your lesson planning to deal more productively with the reading and writing demands of English Language Arts curricula.

## Phase 1: Preteach

- Pull out a manageable number of key concepts.

- Identify vocabulary most critical to talking and learning about the central concepts. Don't attempt to cover all of the vocabulary words you anticipate they will not know. Do more than provide synonyms and definitions. Introduce the essential words in more meaningful contexts, through simple sentences drawing on familiar issues, people, scenarios, and vocabulary. Guide students in articulating the meanings of essential terms through these familiar contexts and hold them responsible for writing the definitions in their own words.

- Present key words when they occur within the context of the reading selection or activity. Make the words as concrete as possible by linking each to an object, photo, drawing, or movement.

- Post the new essential vocabulary in a prominent place in the classroom to create a word bank of organized lesson terminology.

- Examine your lesson to see what types of language functions students will need to participate in various activities. For example, if they are being asked to make predictions about upcoming paragraph content in an essay based on transition words (e.g., *therefore, in addition, consequently*), students will need to be taught some basic sentence patterns and verbs to express opinions (e.g., "I predict that . . ."; "Based on this transition word, I conclude that . . ."). If being asked to agree or disagree with the arguments in a persuasive article, students will need to learn some sentence patterns and verbs to convey agreement or disagreement (e.g., "I don't agree with the author's argument that adolescents don't have a work ethic because . . .").

- Engage students in prereading activities that spark their curiosity and involve them in all four language modes.

- Assess students' prior knowledge related to key concepts through participation structures and collaborative group discussions with realia (e.g., photographs, objects) serving as a visual trigger.

- Utilize realia and visuals needed to make the concepts less abstract.

- Use multimedia presentations such as CD-ROM and videos

to familiarize students with the plot, characters, and themes of a narrative text prior to reading, but don't use it as a replacement for reading.

- Provide a written and oral synopsis of the key content prior to actually asking students to read a selection if the sentence structures and vocabulary are particularly demanding.

- Use graphic organizers and semantic maps to help students grasp the central content in an accessible manner prior to reading.

- Lead a quick text prereading, or "text tour," focusing student attention on illustrations, chapter title and subtopics, boldfaced words, summary sections, and connection of chapter to theme, previous chapters, activities, and concepts.

- When possible, build in opportunities for "narrow reading," allowing students to read more than one selection on the same topic, to build concept and vocabulary recognition that will support their reading more fluently and confidently.

**Phase 2: Teach**
- Clearly establish a reading purpose for students prior to assigning a manageable amount of text.

- Describe and model strategies for navigating different kinds of text. Provide a convincing rationale for each new strategy and regularly review both the purpose and process.

- Familiarize students with a manageable tool kit of reading comprehension and study strategies, and continue practicing these selective strategies. In this way, students end the school year with a viable approach rather than sporadic practice with a confusing array of new reading behaviors.

- Introduce a new strategy using a text that isn't too difficult in order to build credibility for the strategy and ensure student success. Otherwise, if a selection is too difficult and the strategy fails to deliver for students, they will have little faith in experimenting with the new strategy on future texts.

- Whenever possible, get students physically involved with the page, using highlighters, sticky notes, and a small piece of cardboard or heavy construction paper to focus and guide their reading from one paragraph or column to the next.

- Alternate between teacher-facilitated and student-dominated reading activities.

- Do "think-aloud" reading to model your cognitive and metacognitive strategies and thought processes.

- Assign brief amounts of text at a time, and alternate between oral, paired, and silent reading.

- Guide students through the process of reading and comprehending a passage by reading aloud to them and assisting them in identifying the text organization and establishing a clear reading purpose.

- Allow students to read a passage while listening to an audiotape recorded by a classmate, cross-age tutor, or parent volunteer.

- Have students engage in "repeated readings" of the same brief passage to build word recognition, fluency, and reading rate.

- Provide some form of study guide in order to focus their reading on the critical content and prevent them from getting bogged down with nonessential details and unfamiliar vocabulary. A partially completed outline or graphic organizer is more task-based and manageable than a list of questions to answer, which often results in simple scanning for content without really reading and comprehending material.

- Demonstrate your note-taking process and provide models of effective study notes for students to emulate.

**Phase 3: Assess**
- Prepare both text-based and experientially based questions, which lead students from simply getting the gist of a selection to establishing a personal connection to the lesson content.

- Build in task-based and authentic assessment during every lesson to ensure that ELL students are actually developing greater proficiency with new content and strategies. Quick-writes, drawings, oral and written summaries, and collaborative tasks are generally more productive indicators of lesson comprehension than a closing question/answer session.

- Provide safe opportunities for students to alert you to any learning challenges they are experiencing. Have them submit anonymous written questions (formulated either independently or with a partner) about confusing lesson content and process and then follow up on these points of confusion at the end of class or in the subsequent class session.

- Ask students to end the class session by writing 3–5 outcome statements about their experience in the day's lesson, expressing both new understandings and needs for clarification. (See Chapter 4, on Participation Structures, for a detailed discussion of this formative assessment procedure.)

- Make sure that assessment mirrors the lesson objectives. For example, if you are teaching students how to preread expository text, it isn't relevant to assess using comprehension questions. A more authentic assessment of their ability to apply this strategy would be to provide them with a photocopy of an expository selection and ask them to highlight and label the parts one would read during the actual prereading process. It would be relevant, however, to ask them to identify two reasons for engaging in a text prereading before tackling the entire selection.

- Build in opportunities for students to demonstrate their understandings of texts that draw upon different language and literacy skills: formal and informal writing assignments, posters, small-group tasks, oral presentations, and so on.

- Don't assign tasks to ELLs that require little or no reading or lesson comprehension. For example, don't allow them to simply draw a picture while other students are writing a paragraph. Instead, make sure that you have adequately scaffolded the task and equipped them with a writing frame and model to guide them through the process. While one might argue that this is multimodal and tapping into multiple intelligences, it is actually conveying expectations for their development of academic competence in English.

- Make sure that students understand your assessment criteria in advance. Whenever possible, provide models of student work for them to emulate, along with a non-model that fails to meet the specified assessment criteria. Do not provide exemplars that are clearly outside of their developmental range. While this may be an enriching reading task, it will not serve as a viable model. Save student work that can later serve as a model for ELLs with different levels of academic preparation.

- Develop accessible and relevant rubrics for various tasks and products that are customized to the task rather than generic assessment tools. Introduce a rubric in tandem with exemplars of successful and less productive work to help them internalize the assessment criteria. Guide students in identifying the ways in which sample work does or does not meet established grading criteria.

## Phase 4: Extend

- Consider ways in which students can transfer knowledge and skills gleaned from one assignment/lesson to a subsequent lesson.

- Build in opportunities for students to read a more detailed or challenging selection on the same topic in order to allow them to apply familiar concepts and vocabulary and stretch their literacy muscles.

- Recycle pre- and post-reading tasks regularly, so students can become more familiar with the task process and improve their performance. If they are assailed with curricular novelty, ELLs never have the opportunity to refine their skills and demonstrate improved competence. For example, if you ask them to identify a personality trait of an essential character in a story, then support this observation with relevant details in an expository paragraph, it would make sense to have them write an identical paragraph about another character in the near future.

- Discuss with students ways in which they can apply new vocabulary and language strategies outside of the classroom.

- Praise students' efforts to experiment with new language in class, both in writing and in speaking.

- Demonstrate the applicability of new reading and writing strategies to real-world literacy tasks. Bring in potentially more engaging reading selections that will pique their interest and provide a more compelling rationale for applying a new strategic repertoire. Design periodic writing tasks for an authentic audience other than the teacher: another class, fellow classmates, and so on.

# Chapter 7
# Language Arts Instruction and Less Proficient Learners

## Characteristics of Less Proficient Learners

Every middle-grade classroom has a number of less proficient students, individuals who begin the year one, two, or more years below grade level yet do not qualify for special education services and may not be English Language Learners. It is important to keep in mind that most accommodations made for English learners and special needs students will be helpful for all kinds of diverse learners, including less proficient learners. However, it is worthwhile to briefly examine some of the learner characteristics of less proficient students in comparison to their average achieving peers. An appreciation of these distinctions will provide a useful foundation for understanding the importance of using the various "universal access" strategies described throughout this chapter and incorporated into the Prentice Hall Language Arts program.

## Attention and Memory

Research suggests that underachieving students have difficulty in organizing and categorizing new information during instruction. Typically, less skillful students do not effectively order, classify, and arrange information in meaningful ways during learning, frequently leaving them confused and missing the "big picture." Long-term memory is often adversely affected due to the lack of meaningful connections established and difficulty with noticing how new information relates to prior knowledge. In addition, underprepared students frequently do not know how to focus their attention on the important aspects of a classroom presentation, demonstration, or reading selection. In either case, the intentional use of explicit strategies coupled with interactive review and extension activities can make a significant difference in providing poorly prepared students full access to the Language Arts curriculum.

## Lesson Planning and Instructional Accommodations for Attention and Memory

### Phase 1: Preteach

- Gain attention requesting a simple physical response, e.g., "Everyone, eyes on me please," "Touch under number one," and so forth. Students need to show you they are ready.

- Keep the lesson pace moving along briskly—a "perky not pokey" pace is helpful.

- Clarify or introduce critical "big ideas" or conceptual anchors that the reading or lesson or activity is built around (e.g., an example, a metaphor, a demonstration).

- Use brief choral responses when the answer is short and identical. (e.g. "Everyone, the answer to number one is _____".)

- Use brief partner responses when the answer is open-ended and longer. (E.g., "First readers, tell first coaches the most important new information revealed in the last paragraph".)

- Randomly call upon students to build prior knowledge or raise questions the text may answer after they have had a chance to rehearse or practice with a partner.

- Use graphic organizers, charts, and concept maps to assist students with focusing on critical concepts as well as categorizing and organizing information to be studied/learned.

### Phase 2: Teach

- Engage students in a "read/reflect/discuss/note" cycle of filling out the graphic organizers/concept maps collaboratively as you progress through the reading or lesson.

- Do a brief oral review using partners (e.g., think-write-pair-share) to ensure that all students are firm on the big ideas/critical concepts.

- Cue students to take special note of crucial information and explore why this information is so critical.

- Engage students in the active use or processing of the new information (e.g., paraphrase, give an example, write a response).

- Emphasize connections between new and known information.

- Connect new learning to student's personal experience (e.g., coach students to create analogies or metaphors using prior knowledge).

## Phase 3: Assess

- Ask students to explain their graphic organizer/concept map to a partner. Monitor selected students and determine level of understanding—reteach/provide additional examples as necessary.

- Provide students the opportunity to reorganize, prioritize, and otherwise reflect on the key aspects of the lesson.

- Systematically monitor retention of key information or "big ideas" over time using "quick writes" (brief written summaries to a prompt), random questioning, observing student interactions, written assignments, and so on. Reteach, provide additional examples, invite students to elaborate, and so on, as necessary.

## Phase 4: Extend

- Have students design investigations or projects using the information in new ways.

- Design homework assignments that require students to go beyond the text to apply lessons learned to their lives or to other circumstances.

- Challenge students to organize information in novel ways, come up with different categories, and otherwise elaborate the information being studied.

- Draw explicit connections/prompt students to induce connections between information studied earlier in the term and new ideas encountered in the current reading selection.

## Learning Strategies and Use

Perhaps the most ubiquitous characteristic of less proficient students is their lack of effective and efficient strategies for accomplishing various academic tasks, from writing a persuasive essay to taking notes during a lecture, or responding to a piece of literature. Less skillful students tend to have a very limited repertoire of learning strategies and have little awareness of how to monitor the use of learning strategies during reading, writing, and other academic activities. In contrast, successful learners are active, "strategic," and flexible in their employment of appropriate learning strategies tailored to the demands of a particular academic task or assignment.

Kame'enui and Carnine *(see footnote 1, page 1)* suggest three critical design principles teachers need to keep in mind when addressing the issue of learning strategies with underprepared or diverse learners.

1) Important learning strategies must be made overt, explicit, and conspicuous.

2) Strong verbal and visual support, or "scaffolding" should be provided to ensure that diverse learners understand when, where, and how to use the strategies.

3) Judicious review of new learning strategies is required to allow less prepared students enough practice to incorporate the new strategy into their learning routines.

It is important to note that differences between less proficient students and average achievers in their use of learning strategies is not based on organic or biological differences. In other words, it is their lack of experience and preparation that is the critical difference. Fortunately, less proficient learners are quite capable of acquiring effective learning strategies and significantly improving their academic performance when provided with direct instruction in the "what-why-how-when" of strategy use in a highly focused educational setting.

## Lesson Planning and Instructional Accommodations for Learning Strategies

### Phase 1: Preteach
- Clarify the rationale for learning the new strategy in terms, examples, and results the students value (e.g., Where in school or life would it be useful to know how to write a persuasive essay?).

- Brainstorm for examples of successful strategy usage with interactive tactics such as "give one, get one" (*see pages 23–24*) to involve all students. (E.g., Each student lists as many ideas as possible in 3–4 minutes, and then has 3–5 minutes to compare with a peer and "give one" idea to them as well as "get one" from them to extend their brainstormed list.)

- Provide personal examples of how you have used this strategy to your academic advantage.

- Directly teach any "pre-skills" or prerequisite skills students need to perform the strategy.

### Phase 2: Teach
Explicitly model the use of the strategy, including a significant

focus on thinking aloud during the execution of each step in the strategy.

- Provide students with a brief summary of the strategy steps or an acronym to facilitate retention of the strategy. Example:

  **POWER:** **P**repare, **O**rganize, **W**rite, **E**dit, **R**evise
  (Archer & Gleason 2000)

- Guide students in practicing the strategy using less demanding content that allows students to focus on the new strategy. Gradually transition to more difficult content.

- Break the strategy down into explicit steps, ensuring that students are able to perform each step and combine steps to use the whole strategy.

- Structure partner-mediated practice in which students take turns practicing the strategy and providing feedback to one another (e.g., take turns reading a paragraph or page, and paraphrase the gist in 12 words or less).

## Phase 3: Assess

- Monitor partners during strategy practice to observe competence, areas for review, and so forth.

- Randomly call on students to informally demonstrate strategy knowledge.

- Include explicit use of strategies taught as part of the quiz, paper, report, project, and other formal assessments.

## Phase 4: Extend

- Discuss with students where else in or out of school they could use the strategy.

- Provide extra credit or some other incentive to encourage the use of the strategy in other content area classes.

- After they have gained some degree of mastery, encourage students to modify and otherwise personalize the strategy to better fit their learning style or needs.

## Vocabulary and Reading Fluency

Vocabulary differences between struggling and average students are apparent from the primary years in school, and tend to get worse over time. It is not surprising that less prepared learners engage in far less reading in and out of school, resulting in substantially impoverished vocabularies.

In addition, their ability to read fluently and accurately is often diminished, further compounding the issue and rendering reading a frustrating and defeating experience.

There is no short cut or "quick fix" for vocabulary building, but teachers can make a tremendous difference by sustained attention to the following practices:

- Directly teaching key conceptual vocabulary using strategies that take students beyond simple memorization

- Teaching students how to learn words and concepts from context

- Encouraging wide reading in and out of school. Students who have serious fluency problems (e.g., reading below 100 words per minute in grade-level text) will require sustained practice daily in repeated reading of instructional level/age-appropriate texts.

### Lesson Planning and Instructional Accommodations for Vocabulary and Fluency

**Phase 1: Preteach**
- Select conceptually rich, critical vocabulary for more detailed instruction before reading.

- Choose age- and level-appropriate passages for students to use repeated reading strategies (e.g., on prerecorded tapes, partner reading, choral reading w/small groups).

**Phase 2: Teach**
- Directly teach the meanings of critical, conceptually rich vocabulary required for full understanding of the passage or lesson.

- Pick vocabulary strategies that take students beyond simple repetition of the definition to prompt active construction of new connections between the concept and their prior knowledge. Such strategies include
—creating semantic maps showing how words are related.
—using the words in sentences that "show you know" the meaning.
—defining the critical attributes of the concept in short bulleted phrases.

- Create examples and non-examples of the concept, prompting students to explain why or why not the exemplar has the attributes of the concept under consideration (a graphic organizer showing the attributes and examples/non-examples can be very useful).

- Engage students in word sorts: Provide 10–20 vocabulary words for students to place into preset categories (e.g., parts of speech, descriptive of the character or not, and so on).

- Pair students at similar instructional levels for repeated reading practice; have the more proficient student read a paragraph to a page, and then have the less proficient student reread the same section.

- Practice repeated reading of instructional level passages of 150–200 words in length with prerecorded tapes, set goals, and individually graph and monitor fluency daily, finishing with a written retelling of the passage.

- Teach students important generative word roots (e.g., Latin and Greek) and common affixes. Practice sorting and combining to examine how they work (e.g., spec: *spectrum, spectacle, inspection, speculation*).

- Model and practice the use of context in predicting word meanings during reading, thinking aloud to demonstrate to students how textual cues direct your thinking.

## Phase 3: Assess

- Randomly call on students to provide examples of the vocabulary word under examination.
- Monitor students during partner discussion of selected critical vocabulary words.
- Evaluate students during small group discussion, written products, and so on.
- Directly monitor the fluency of selected students via one-minute timings. Note rate, accuracy, and expression.

## Phase 4: Extend

- Encourage students to informally use recently taught vocabulary words in "show you know" sentences during classroom conversations, written products, and so on.

- Intentionally revisit newly acquired vocabulary during discussion, while thinking aloud during demonstrations, and so on.

- Encourage students to practice fluency building via repeated reading at home, appropriate CD-ROM technology, and cross-age tutoring of younger students, in which the target student must prepare a story to fluency for use with his or her tutee.

## Motivation and Academic Identity

Motivation is complex and difficult to define, but most experts agree it is significantly related to how much success or failure one has experienced relative to the activity in question. Less proficient middle-grade students typically do not see themselves as capable of sustained reading, inquiry, or writing in a challenging academic setting. The old cliché "Nothing succeeds like success" is relevant to this discussion. To build motivation and encourage the development of a productive "academic identity," it is important to engage less proficient students in challenging lessons while simultaneously incorporating adequate support or instructional scaffolding to increase the likelihood students will experience success. In addition, helping students to explore their thinking as they read and write through structured dialogues and thinking aloud can be very helpful. Noted reading researcher David Pearson calls this process a "metacognitive conversation," allowing less proficient students to gain an understanding of how successful readers and writers think as they work. In a manner of speaking, teachers can provide less proficient students with an academic or cognitive role model. For example, modeling a simple self-monitoring strategy during writing such as "remember your audience" can assist students in keeping multiple perspectives in mind as they compose.

## Lesson Planning and Instructional Accommodations for Motivation and Academic Identity

Motivation and academic identity do not lend themselves to the Preteach, Teach, Assess, and Extend lesson format. In a sense, motivation is more "caught than taught" and will be the result of successfully engaging students in the curriculum. However, there are a number of general strategies that are useful to consider including:

- **Self-selected reading.** Allow less proficient students regular opportunities to read material they are interested in, at their instructional level.

- **Goal setting.** Engage students in setting personal goals for various academic tasks such as pages/chapters read per week, strategy usage, words read per minute during fluency practice, and so forth.

- **Metacognitive dialogues.** Ask students to informally share their perceptions, approaches, and fears regarding various school-related challenges. Students and teachers then share their thoughts and feelings about how they used various strategies to become more successful.

- **Book clubs, book reviews, newsletter reviews, e-mail postings.** These provide an audience for students' opinions about books they have read.

- **Partnerships** between students and with younger students, community members and business personnel.

- **Negotiated choices.** As appropriate, involve students in negotiating alternative assignments, options, and novel ideas to reach common goals.

- **Model an "academic identity."** Teachers/students/other adults invited into the classroom share how they developed as literate citizens.

## Summary

Less proficient middle-grade students are underprepared for the academic challenges of a rigorous grade-level Language Arts program in a variety of ways. Many of their difficulties can be linked to difficulties with attention and memory, learning strategies, vocabulary and reading fluency, and motivation/academic identity. Middle-grade Language Arts teachers can have an extremely beneficial effect on the learning of less proficient students by the sustained focus on appropriate strategies for preteaching, teaching, assessment, and extension beyond the lesson.

# Chapter 8
# Language Arts Instruction and Students With Special Education Needs

Students with special education needs are a highly diverse student group. Although their learning needs vary greatly, a majority of children identified as special education students will experience mild to severe difficulties in becoming proficient and independent readers and writers. Through instruction that incorporates adaptations and modifications and is delivered in collaborative ways, students with disabilities can gain literacy skills and be active participants in general education language arts curriculum and instruction.

## Characteristics of Special Education Learners

### Eligibility for Special Education

Federal law IDEA '97 (Individuals with Disabilities Education Act, P.L. 105–17) specifies disabling conditions under which students are found eligible to receive special education services. These disabling conditions may be clustered into the two broad categories of high incidence and low incidence disabilities (see box for descriptions of disabling conditions). Each student with a disability may experience specific cognitive, communicative, behavioral/social/emotional, physical, and learning issues. Students may exhibit all, or some combination, of the characteristics listed for their particular disability, and in the case of some students, have more than one disability (e.g., a student identified as having a learning disability may also have a communicative disorder). Because of the heterogeneity of the special education student population, even within categories of disability, an Individualized Education Program (IEP) is created for each student found eligible to receive special education services.

## Disabling Conditions

| High Incidence Disabilities | Descriptors | Reading Instruction Consideration |
|---|---|---|
| • *Speech or Language Impairment* | • Speech disorders include difficulties in articulation, voice, and fluency.<br><br>• Language impairments may include difficulties in phonology, morphology, syntax, semantics, and pragmatics. | • When possible, provide opportunities for intensive instruction in decoding and word-recognition skills (e.g., computer drill and practice programs; flash cards of frequently encountered words).<br><br>• Provide time for students to read the text multiple times to gain fluency (e.g., repeated readings; paired reading).<br><br>• Explicitly teach vocabulary and teach students strategies for dealing with unknown words (e.g., teaching syllabification skills; teaching meaning of prefixes and suffixes).<br><br>• Explicitly teach more complex language patterns (e.g., compound sentences) and literary elements (e.g., idioms, metaphors). |
| • *Learning Disabilities* | • Students exhibit average to above-average intelligence combined with uneven academic performance patterns (i.e., perform at an average to above-average level in some academic subjects, while experiencing significant difficulties in others).<br><br>• Students experience processing difficulties (e.g., have difficulty taking in oral and print information and in expressing ideas orally and in writing).<br><br>• Students may experience attention and social/behavioral challenges. | • Preteach "big ideas" and vocabulary.<br><br>• Provide multiple opportunities for students to read text to gain fluency.<br><br>• Explicitly teach vocabulary using activities that are multisensory and require active participation (e.g., acting out meaning of words; drawing images to represent word meanings; tape-recording words and word meanings; using computer software programs).<br><br>• Explicitly teach comprehension strategies by modeling the steps, guiding the students through the steps, and monitoring for implementation (e.g., webbing and outlining; predicting; summarizing).<br><br>• Provide multiple avenues for demonstrating compre-hension of text (e.g., writing, drawing, speaking, acting out scenes). |
| • *Emotional Disturbance* | • Students experience difficulty learning that is not due to cognitive, sensory, or health factors.<br><br>• Students may have difficulty forging and maintaining interpersonal relationships. | • Make students accountable during large group, small group, and paired reading (e.g., have them take notes and make and check predictions; ask questions of all group members, not just a spokesperson; have students complete individual quizzes to check for understanding). |

| | | |
|---|---|---|
| | • Students may display inappropriate behaviors or feelings under normal circumstances.<br>• Students may experience feelings of unhappiness or depression.<br>• Students may have physical symptoms or fears associated with personal or school problems. | • Explicitly teach skills for working in groups (e.g., how to ask questions; how to state an opinion; how to disagree with another person's ideas).<br>• Provide structure and establish routines for reading activities and transitions (e.g., specify expectations during large group reading; establish routines for how students are to complete comprehension activities).<br>• Become familiar with the student's behavior plan and systematically implement it in the classroom (e.g., use the reinforcers and consequences identified in the plan to build consistency for the student). |
| • *Mental Retardation* | • Students will demonstrate subaverage (in students with mild/moderate mental-retardation) to significantly subaverage (in students with severe mental retardation) intellectual functioning.<br>• Students will demonstrate overall low performance in adaptive behavior domains (e.g., taking care of personal health needs). | • Preteach and reteach vocabulary and concepts as needed.<br>• Make concepts concrete by linking concepts to the students' daily lives.<br>• Explicitly model what is expected, and when able, provide examples of completed projects.<br>• Provide multiple avenues for students to engage with text (e.g., books on tape, paired reading, passages in hypertext format).<br>• Provide multiple exposures to the same text and its key vocabulary.<br>• Provide multiple ways for students to demonstrate understanding of text. |
| • *Low Incidence Disabilities* | **Note:** *Students with low incidence disabilities may have average to above-average intelligence, or may experience cognitive impairments ranging from mild to severe.* | **Note:** *Students with low incidence disabilities may have average to above- average intelligence, or may experience cognitive impairments ranging from mild to severe.* |
| • *Deaf/Hard of Hearing* | • Students who are deaf or who have some degree of hearing loss | • Present ideas visually.<br>• Capture key ideas from discussions in written form on the overhead or chalk board.<br>• Use FMI systems when available.<br>• When orally reading text, reduce background noise as much as possible; when conducting small group or paired reading activities, consider having the groups move to other rooms or spaces.<br>• Work with the interpreter or special education staff to identify adaptations and modifications. |

| | | |
|---|---|---|
| • *Blind/Low Vision* | • Students who are blind or who have some vision | • Present ideas auditorily and through tactile modes to support student access.<br>• Work with the special education teacher to secure large-print text, brailled text, books on tape, and AAC reading devices.<br>• Work with the special education staff to identify specific adaptations and modifications. |
| • *Deaf/ Blindness* | • Students who have concomitant hearing and visual impairments | • Work with the special education staff to identify specific adaptations and modifications.<br>• Gain understanding and a level of comfort in using the AAC devices the student is using in the classroom. |
| • *Other Health Impaired* | • Students with health conditions that limit strength, vitality, or alertness (e.g., heart condition, sickle cell anemia, epilepsy, AIDS) | • Work with the special education staff to identify adaptations and modifications.<br>• Gain understanding of the child's condition and day-to-day and emergency medical needs.<br>• Develop plans for dealing with students' absences. |
| • *Orthopedic Disabilities* | • Students with physical disabilities (e.g., club-foot, bone tuberculosis, cerebral palsy) | • Work with the special education staff to identify specific adaptations and modifications.<br>• Work with the special education staff to secure adapted materials and AAC devices, as appropriate (e.g., book holder; computer voice recognition system that allows student to dictate written assignments).<br>• Adapt routines and activities to take into consideration the student's physical needs (e.g., room arrangement that allows for mobility in a wheelchair; procedures for distributing and collecting materials; procedures for forming work groups.) |
| • *Autism* | • Students experience difficulty in verbal and nonverbal communication<br>• Students experience difficulties in social interactions<br>• Is commonly referred to as a "spectrum disorder" because of the heterogeneity of the group | • Work with the special education staff to identify specific adaptations and modifications.<br>• Structure group and paired activities to take into consideration the child's needs; teach social skills and supports for working in small group and paired situations.<br>• Connect concepts and vocabulary to the interests of the student.<br>• Work with the special education staff to implement behavioral/social plans to provide consistency.<br>• Establish and maintain routines to ensure predictability within the classroom. |

| • Traumatic Brain Injury | • Students who experience an acquired injury to the brain<br><br>• Injury results in total or partial functional disability or psychological impairment (e.g., cognition, language, memory, attention, reasoning) | • Work with the special education staff to identify specific adaptations and modifications.<br><br>• Adapt routines and activities to take into consideration the student's physical needs (e.g., room arrangement that allows for mobility in a wheelchair).<br><br>• Take into consideration student's language, memory, and attention skill needs when constructing class assignments and activities.<br><br>• Preteach and reteach concepts and vocabulary as appropriate. |
| --- | --- | --- |

## Individualized Education Plan

The IEP serves to guide general and special education teachers, related service providers, and parents in designing and delivering educational programs that maximize students' school participation and learning. The IEP includes goals, objectives, and benchmarks that outline what an individual student is expected to learn and achieve during the course of the academic year, as well as the types of services and special adaptations and modifications that are to be put into place to support the educational achievement of the student. For example, in the area of language arts instruction, a student's IEP may include the following goal and objectives:

Goal: Jamal will improve in reading comprehension skills as measured by the district-adopted standardized test.

Objective: Given narrative passages written at the seventh-grade level, Jamal will correctly write the name(s) of the main character(s) and outline, in writing, the main events of the passages in correct sequence for three out of four passages by December.

Objective: Given expository passages written at the seventh-grade level, Jamal will correctly write the main idea of the passages and at least three supporting details for three out of four passages by February.

The IEP goes on to identify specific services the student will need in order to achieve these goals and objectives. A range of services is available to students with disabilities through their IEP. Services fall along a continuum and include the option of students receiving instruction in general education classrooms with special education supports and participating in specialized instruction delivered by special education teachers in special education classrooms for one or more periods a day. The type of service delivery to be provided is determined individually for each student through the IEP meeting. The general education teacher, in partnership with the special education staff and the student's parents, and when appropriate, the student, determine the type of service delivery that is most appropriate for a student based on his/her learning needs.

Many students with disabilities are educated in general education classrooms alongside their general education peers. Service-delivery models that support student participation in general education classrooms go by various names, including mainstreaming, integration, and inclusion. All have the under-lying same intent—to provide for the needs of students with disabilities in their least restrictive environment, alongside their general education peers.

In the case of Jamal, the service delivery option selected and specified in his IEP may look something like this:

Student will participate in the general education language arts class and in one period of special education reading resource support each day. The special education teacher will team with the general education language arts teacher at least two days per week to provide instruction in the general education language arts class.

IEPs also specify the types of curricular, instructional, and behavioral adaptations and modifications that are to be put into place to support the student's achievement. For Jamal, the follow-ing adaptations and modifications may be specified in the IEP:

The student will receive instruction in learning strategies to identify characters, story sequence, and main ideas and supporting details. The student will be provided a story map for identifying the main character(s) and for sequencing story events. The student will be provided a main idea/supporting details map when working with expository passages.

The IEP is a guide that details the types of goals, educational program, and adaptations and modifications a special education student is to receive. The IEP is developed by a team and is reviewed at least annually. General education teachers, special education professionals, administrators, parents, and students all have a voice in the development of the individual IEP.

## Lesson Planning and Instructional Accommodations

When developing language arts lesson plans for inclusive classrooms of general and special education learners, teachers will want to consider the addition of teaching and learning strategies that will support universal access to the content. Teachers will need to be familiar with the unique learning needs and requirements of the students and their goals, objectives and benchmarks and, through collaboration with other IEP team members, incorporate those needs and strategies into the classroom.

This process does not need to be as intimidating as it sounds because there are some common, relatively unintrusive teaching and learning strategies that can be implemented in the classroom to address students' specific needs, as well as support the learning of the other students present in the classroom. For example, students with disabilities can greatly benefit from activities that preteach and reteach concepts, that explicitly link lesson content with prior experience and knowledge, that directly teach the meaning of critical vocabulary words, and that explicitly model how tasks are to be completed. This is true for other learners as well, including less proficient readers and students who are English language learners. Lesson plans that include explicit instruction in behavioral and social expectations also help to ensure student participation and learning. Pacing is also an issue. Some students with disabilities will require a somewhat slower pace or an ongoing review of key concepts if they are to grasp key understandings and skills. Also, activities need to be considered in light of the students' disabilities. For example, will special materials be needed (such as materials with enlarged print for students with low vision, or adapted manipulatives that can be used by a student with a physical disability)? If participating in student-mediated instruction (e.g., small group learning), what type of preparation will students receive for participating in these activities? Will the activities provide necessary supports to ensure student participation (e.g., will directions be explicit and in writing as well as presented verbally)?

There are a number of other simple adaptations and modifications general education teachers can implement in the classroom to directly address the literacy learning needs of students with disabilities. In fact, in many cases, these adaptations and modifications will assist all learners in the classroom, including typically developing readers, English learners, and less proficient readers. A beginning list of suggestions for meaningfully including students with disabilities in the general education language arts curriculum are presented in the box. Although presented in terms of disabling conditions, the suggestions apply across conditions.

It is also helpful to think of instructional considerations that specifically apply to the four phases of instruction: Preteach, Teach, Assess, and Extend. A beginning list of suggestions is provided below.

## Phase 1: Preteach

- Identify the most critical and high-utility vocabulary words for comprehension of the passage. Provide explicit instruction in the meaning of these words that incorporates instruction in the understanding of prefixes, suffixes, root words, synonyms, and antonyms.

- Provide an overview of key ideas and concepts presented in the text using study guides, outlines, or maps.

- Explicitly connect text content with the students' lives.

- Preteach key concepts.

## Phase 2: Teach

- Present all ideas orally and visually, and when possible, incorporate tactile and kinesthetic experiences as well.

- Stop often to discuss key ideas and check for understanding.

- Limit the presentation of information or discussion of key topics to short periods of time (no more than ten minutes) to enhance attention.

- Require students to demonstrate that they are listening and following along (e.g., taking notes, running a finger along the text).

- Incorporate active reading strategies (e.g., choral reading, paired reading) to assist students in maintaining attention.

- Be sure to provide necessary adaptive materials as appropriate (e.g., enlarged print).

- Incorporate the same comprehension and learning strategies over extended periods to allow for mastery. This will provide students with multiple opportunities to practice a strategy and to become comfortable in its application. This will also prevent "strategy clutter" that can occur when a student has too many strategies to draw from and is not facile enough with any to allow for ease of use.

- Provide specific and step-by-step instructions. Model what the students are to do, step-by-step.

### Phase 3: Assess
- Go beyond questioning techniques to assess students' understanding by having them write questions about what they have learned, identify those sections they find are unclear or confusing, or complete short writes of the key points.

- When having students work in groups or pairs, set up procedures that maintain individual student accountability (e.g., students each having to write, draw, or state a response).

- When appropriate, have students self-manage and chart their performance. Academic performance, homework and assignment completion, and behavior could be charted.

### Phase 4: Extend
- Provide examples of completed projects.

- Allow students to work in pairs or small groups.

- Provide outlines of what is to be done, with suggested dates and timelines for project completion.

### Collaboration as a Key to Student Achievement

One of the most critical things a general education teacher can do is to collaborate with the special education teachers and staff. Special education staff have extensive expertise in working with students with disabilities and are there to support each student with an IEP. These professionals are available as support systems for general education teachers and parents. The chart *(See pages 60–61)* presents a brief list of potential special educators that you may want to contact when working with students with disabilities in your general education classroom.

General education teachers can do a great deal to ensure that students with disabilities are meaningfully included in the life of the classroom. The following attributes are important to all classrooms but play a key role in the creation of a classroom culture and climate that supports the participation and achievement of students with disabilities:

- Exploring differences and the importance of the acceptance of differences
- Setting clear expectations for all students that take into consideration students' learning styles and needs
- Providing students with reasonable choices
- Setting up instructional activities that foster the development of relationships between students, and between students and teachers
- Demonstrating mutual respect, fairness, and trust

For example, in the case of Jamal, you could work with the special education teacher to identify those learning strategies you are already teaching in the classroom that will assist Jamal. You may want to invite the special education teacher into the classroom to provide instruction in other critical learning strategies that would assist all of your students in becoming better readers and writers, including Jamal. Because Jamal is receiving resource-room support one period per day, you may want to discuss with the special education teacher the type of instruction he is receiving during the support period, and together work to develop a plan that links the curriculum of the two learning environments. You will most likely be involved in assessing whether Jamal is achieving his goals and objectives and in providing instruction to support their achievement.

## Summary

Students with disabilities are a highly heterogeneous group of learners. Their cognitive and behavioral, social, and physical needs can present unique challenges in the classroom, but through careful and strategic planning and collaboration among professionals and parents, these students can be contributing and vital members of the classroom community, as well as readers and writers. It is the professionals' responsibility, in consultation with the parents, to ensure universal access to the curriculum for these students. Lesson planning and the inclusion of adaptations and modifications within lessons are beginning points for achieving the goal of universal access for students with disabilities.

# Special Education Teachers and Service Providers

| Support Provider | Roles | How They Can Support the General Education Teacher |
|---|---|---|
| Special Education Teacher • resource teacher • itinerant teacher • special-day class teacher • inclusion specialist | • Is intimately familiar with students' IEP goals, objectives/benchmarks, and the students' academic, communicative, and behavioral/emotional needs<br>• Has expertise in how to adapt and modify curriculum and instruction to meaningfully include students with disabilities in general education classrooms and curriculum<br>• Has expertise for providing remedial support and intensive intervention services for students with disabilities | • Can answer questions about students' learning needs<br>• Can explain the students' IEP and what can be done in the general education class to support student achievement of IEP goals and objectives/benchmarks<br>• Can help you develop ways to adapt and modify instruction that will help students learn<br>• Can work with you in the classroom to support the students' participation and achievement |
| Para-professional | • May be assigned to "shadow" a student in the general education classroom<br>• Can assist in adapting and modifying curriculum and instruction for the particular student(s)<br>• May serve to monitor student's academic and behavioral/emotional needs and intervention plans<br>• May assist students in meeting physical, mobility, and health needs | • Can assist you in addressing the student's needs (e.g., can provide that one-on-one explanation that you may not be able to get to because of the other students in the classroom)<br>• Can be responsible for adapting and modifying instructional activities and assignments, with guidance from you and the special education teachers<br>• Can oversee the implementation of specialized intervention plans<br>• Can be responsible for student's physical, mobility, and health needs |
| Audiologist | • Expertise in measuring students' hearing levels and evaluating hearing loss | • Can give you suggestions for how to work with students who have partial or total hearing loss<br>• Can give you suggestions for how to deal with a student who refuses to wear his/her hearing aids in class |

| | | |
|---|---|---|
| Physical and Occupational Therapist | • Physical therapist generally focuses on gross motor development (e.g., walking, running)<br><br>• Occupational therapist generally focuses on fine motor development (e.g., using writing tools) | • Can give you suggestions for how to modify requirements to take into consideration students' motor and physical needs |
| School or Educational Psychologist | • Expertise in educational testing administration and interpretation<br><br>• May also have training in counseling and working with students in crisis situations | • Can help you understand testing results and may be able to come into the classroom to observe and give you suggestions for working with a particular student<br><br>• Can help you work with a student who is in crisis (e.g., divorce, death) |
| Augmentative and Alternative Communicative Specialist | • Expertise in assessing students' AAC needs<br><br>• Expertise in developing programs that assist students in using alternative means for communicating verbally and in writing (e.g., commnication boards, using speech synthesizer software) | • Can explain to you how a student's AAC device works<br><br>• Can give you suggestions for how to make adaptations and modifications that support the student's use of the AAC device in the classroom (e.g., physical arrangement of the learning environment; assignment adjustments) |
| Educational Therapist | • Expertise in assessment and remediation for students experiencing learning problems<br><br>• May serve as a case manager and build commu- nicative links between school, home, and related service providers | • Can give you suggestions for how to adapt instruction to meet the student's needs<br><br>• Can give you suggestions for communicating with parents and for working with the special education staff |

# Chapter 9
# Summary

The middle-grade classroom of today is more diverse than ever before, posing considerable challenges to teachers, curriculum developers, and school administrators as they strive to design programs to ensure that all students reach ambitious grade-level standards. Teachers are faced with the daunting task of teaching students how to transform massive amounts of information into knowledge that can be used to solve increasingly complex academic problems *(see footnote 1 on page 1)*. There is clearly no panacea or silver bullet solution to the question of how to best meet the varied learning needs found in today's middle-grade Language Arts classroom. To be certain, some students will need additional tutoring, English language development, and specialized services to reach their full learning potential. However, the lesson design format of Preteach, Teach, Assess, and Extend coupled with the instructional strategies and teaching tactics described within this document constitute a viable framework for working with these challenges in the core Language Arts classroom.

For example, the notion of "front-loading" instruction via a concentrated focus on explicitly teaching critical conceptual vocabulary, clarifying big ideas, and pre-reading, considered "best practice" for typical middle-grade classrooms, becomes a prerequisite for success in an inclusive classroom. Differentiating instruction to provide the right balance of scaffolded support and demand for rigor is a balancing act. Some students will need two or three additional examples to really "get it," while those with more extensive prior knowledge deserve challenges that take them beyond the first example to create novel exemplars of their own. In either case, the heart of the matter involves being clear on what is to be learned, assessing students' prior knowledge, and selecting instructional strategies that match need. Certainly, this is far easier to say than to do. Nevertheless, in school after school, when teachers engage in collaborative efforts across labels and categories enhanced by sustained professional development linked to ambitious standards, the resultant student achievement is indeed impressive.

When all is said and done, the key to successful teaching in a highly diverse, inclusive middle-grade classroom requires teachers to balance the needs of the head with those of the heart. In other words, it means combining the affective needs of adolescents for community, connection to peers, feelings of acceptance and safety, and honoring individual differences within an intellectually thoughtful and rigorous curriculum. Classroom diversity is a little like a two-edged sword, exacting academic challenge while at the same time presenting a rich palette within which to more fully bring the Language Arts to life.

# Appendix
# Instructional Resources for Diverse English Language Arts Classrooms

## English Language Learners

Bates, L., Lane, J., & Lange, E. (1993). *Writing Clearly: Responding to ESL Compositions.* Heinle & Heinle.

Peregoy, S., & Boyle, O. (1997). *Reading, Writing, and Learning in ESL: A Resource Book for K-12 Teachers,* Second Edition. Longman.

Spangenberg-Urbschat, K., & Pritchard, R. (Eds.). (1994). *Kids Come in all Languages: Reading Instruction for ESL Students.* International Reading Association.

## Vocabulary

Allen, J. (1999). *Words, Words, Words: Teaching Vocabulary in Grades 4–12.* Stenhouse.

Blachowicz, C., & Fisher, P. (1996). *Teaching Vocabulary in all Classrooms.* Merrill/Prentice Hall.

## Participation

Harmin, M. (1995). *Strategies to Inspire Active Learning.* Inspiring Strategy Institute.

Kagan, S. (1992). *Cooperative Learning.* Kagan Cooperative Learning.

## Special Needs Learners

McCarney, S.B. (1988). *The Pre-referral Intervention Manual.* Columbia, OH: Hawthorne.

## Web Resources

Council on Exceptional Children
http://www.cec.sped.org Produced by the largest special education advocacy and support organization, this site is loaded with resources, links, answers to questions, resources for parents/teachers and more.

Learning Disabilities Online
> http://www.ldonline.org
> One of the premier Web sites for reading problems, attention issues, and related challenges. Many practical teaching resources, video, lesson plans, and more.

Charles Schwab Educational Foundation
> http://www.schwablearning.org
> An excellent resource for teachers, parents, and professionals of any field interested in learning disabilities.

University of Northern Iowa—Inclusion Support
> http://www.uni.edu/coe/inclusion
> A gold mine of resources for teachers, assistants, parents, administrators, and others interested in inclusion.

## Reading and Language Arts

National Reading Panel
> http://www.nationalreadingpanel.org/
> Commissioned by Congress, the NRP reviewed over 115,000 studies related to the teaching of reading and has synthesized the results in a very user-friendly document, video, and practical application booklet full of useful strategies (available free online or call 800-370-2943).

International Reading Association
> http://www.ira.org/
> The largest professional organization dedicated to promoting reading and literacy in our country.

Reading Online
> http://www.readingonline.org/
> A useful resource for practical articles, strategies, and tactics to support teachers.

National Research Center of English Learning and Achievement
> http://cela.albany.edu/mission.htm
> The only national center funded by the Department of Education to support teachers of English Language Arts.

California Online Resources for Educators
> http://www.sdcoe.k12.ca.us/score/cyberguide.html
> Produces CyberGuides, supplementary, standards-based, Web-delivered units of instruction centered on core works of literature K–12.

Computer Based Study Strategies
http://npip.com/CBSS/cbss.htm
Using computers as a "cognitive partner," CBSS is loaded with practical ideas, lesson plans, links for inexpensive mapping and writing software and more.

California Dept of Education—Language Arts
http://www.cde.ca.gov/ci/lh.html
Many useful resources, including a book very helpful to middle-grade Language Arts teachers: *Strategic Teaching and Learning: Standards-Based Instruction to Promote Content Literacy in Grades Four Through Twelve.*